Ethnic and Racial Minorities in Asia

I0128952

Ethnic and Racial Minorities in Asia explores the relationship between ethnic minority rights and citizenship in Asia. Occupying a prominent place on the global map of conflict, Asia is one of the most ethnically diverse and racially divided regions in the world. It is also the scene of some of the most contrasting state responses to ethnic and racial conflicts, ranging from violent military repression and coercion on the one hand, to offers of autonomy and other forms of self-rule aimed at granting minorities more equal and inclusive citizenship on the other hand.

This volume combines conceptual debates about citizenship with case studies of ethnic minorities from across the Asian region, with a particular emphasis on Southeast Asia. The contributing authors question the nature of citizenship in the broader sense of identity, belonging, and the rights and responsibilities of ethnic minorities in relation to sovereign nation-states. They examine a wide range of key issues including minority rights claims, ethnic and racial conflict, citizenship, constructions and representations of identity, post-colonialism and human security.

This book was originally published as a special issue of *Ethnic and Racial Studies*.

Michelle Ann Miller is a Research Fellow at the Asia Research Institute, National University of Singapore. She previously taught at Deakin University and Charles Darwin University. Michelle is the author of *Rebellion and Reform in Indonesia* (2009), and has published articles and book chapters on decentralization, minority rights, the politics of Islamic law, urban-rural relations and conflict-related issues.

Ethnic and Racial Studies
Series editors: Martin Bulmer and John Solomos, *University of Surrey, UK*

The journal *Ethnic and Racial Studies* was founded in 1978 by John Stone to provide an international forum for high quality research on race, ethnicity, nationalism and ethnic conflict. At the time the study of race and ethnicity was still a relatively marginal sub-field of sociology, anthropology and political science. In the intervening period the journal has provided a space for the discussion of core theoretical issues, key developments and trends, and for the dissemination of the latest empirical research.

It is now the leading journal in its field and has helped to shape the development of scholarly research agendas. *Ethnic and Racial Studies* attracts submissions from scholars in a diverse range of countries, fields of scholarship and crosses disciplinary boundaries. It has moved from being a quarterly to being published monthly and it is now available in both printed and electronic form.

The Ethnic and Racial Studies book series contains a wide range of the journal's special issues. These special issues are an important contribution to the work of the journal, where leading social science academics bring together articles on specific themes and issues that are linked to the broad intellectual concerns of *Ethnic and Racial Studies*. The series editors work closely with the guest editors of the special issues to ensure that they meet the highest quality standards possible. Through publishing these special issues as a series of books, we hope to allow a wider audience of both scholars and students from across the social sciences to engage with the work of *Ethnic and Racial Studies*.

The Transnational Political Participation of Immigrants
Edited by Jean-Michel Lafleur and Marco Martiniello

Anthropology of Migration and Multiculturalism
Edited by Steven Vertovec

Migrant Politics and Mobilisation: Exclusion, Engagements, Incorporation
Edited by Davide Però and John Solomos

Ethnic and Racial Minorities in Asia

Inclusion or Exclusion?

Edited by
Michelle Ann Miller

Routledge
Taylor & Francis Group
LONDON AND NEW YORK

First published 2012
by Routledge
2 Park Square, Milton Park, Abingdon, Oxon, OX14 4RN

Simultaneously published in the USA and Canada
by Routledge
605 Third Avenue, New York, NY 10017

Routledge is an imprint of the Taylor & Francis Group, an informa business

First issued in paperback 2013

This book is a reproduction of *Ethnic and Racial Studies*, volume 34, issue 5. The Publisher requests to those authors who may be citing this book to state, also, the bibliographical details of the special issue on which the book was based.

British Library Cataloguing in Publication Data
A catalogue record for this book is available from the British Library

ISBN13: 978-0-415-67713-4 (hbk)
ISBN13: 978-0-415-84853-4 (pbk)

Typeset in Times New Roman
by Taylor and Francis Books

Disclaimer
The publisher would like to make readers aware that the chapters in this book are referred to as articles as they had been in the special issue. The publisher accepts responsibility for any inconsistencies that may have arisen in the course of preparing this volume for print.

Contents

Notes on Contributors

Jacques Bertrand is Associate Professor of Political Science at the University of Toronto, Canada.

Stefan Ehrentraut is a PhD candidate at the University of Potsdam, Germany.

Damien Kingsbury is Professor in the School of International and Political Studies at Deakin University, Australia.

Gabriele Marranci is Associate Professor in the Department of Sociology at the National University of Singapore and an Associate Professor (Honorary Senior Fellow) at the Centre for the Study of Islam, Cardiff University, UK.

Duncan McCargo is Professor of Southeast Asian Politics at the University of Leeds, UK.

Michelle Ann Miller is a Research Fellow in the Asia Research Institute at the National University of Singapore.

Ethnic minorities in Asia: inclusion or exclusion?

Michelle Ann Miller

Abstract

This special issue, devoted to ethnic minorities in Asia, originated with the *International Symposium on Ethnic Minorities in Asia: Subjects or Citizens*, held at the Asia Research Institute, National University of Singapore. As one of the most ethnically-diverse regions in the world, Asia is the site of large indigenous minority populations as well as non-indigenous minorities through ever-growing legal and illegal migrant flows. This article maps out some of the key themes explored by the contributors to this special issue in the processes and structures of accommodation for Asia's minorities. These themes revolve around the changing meaning of citizenship in Asian contexts, state models of accommodation, constructions and representations of identity and belonging, post-colonial legacies and nation-building, the legitimacy of minority rights claims, and questions of human security. This article provides an overview of the theoretical and empirical contributions that the essays in this special issue bring to the study of ethnic minority issues in increasingly heterogeneous and divided Asian societies.

The engagement by nation-states with their ethnic minority popula-tions normatively involves notions of citizenship and the applicability of universal human rights norms and values in addressing minority concerns. In Asia, growing ethnic diversity and racial conflict over recent years has prompted national governments in the region to rethink their programmes and priorities in dealing with minority issues. Across Southeast Asia in particular, the initiation of national democratization processes since the 1990s has ushered in new regimes and political leaders who have begun to look beyond repressive and coercive strategies to manage minority assertions of difference and towards more inclusive forms of democratic accommodation. Such democratic reforms have typically emphasized the conferral of more equal or greater rights and freedoms to ethnic minorities, including – in some cases – increased possibilities for the attainment of full and equal citizenship.

At the same time, other Asian states have resisted pressure by liberal democratic civil society forces and sections of the international community to adopt more inclusive policies towards their ethnic minorities by pursuing exclusionary nation-building projects based on uniform, majoritarian forms of citizenship. For authoritarian regimes and military dictatorships, the denial or confinement of ethnic diversity to the symbolic realm has often served to legitimize their continued rule by discrediting institutions and agendas not ratified by the state. Undemocratic governments in Asia and elsewhere have also benefitted from ethnic and racial conflict by using the pretext of social disharmony to impose rigid forms of nationalism that privilege and reinforce the hegemony of the ethnic majority (see, for example, Robison 1993, p. 42; Santamaria 2004, p. 8; Miller 2009, pp. 43–4; Thio 2010, p. 100).

The contributors to this special issue came together at the *International Symposium on Ethnic Minorities in Asia: Subjects or Citizens?*, convened at the Asia Research Institute, National University of Singapore on 25–26 June 2009. They considered important questions about the rights and responsibilities of Asian governments in dealing with their ethnic minority populations. What does the status of 'citizen' mean for Asia's ethnic minorities, and to what extent do minorities become 'subjects' when their civil and political rights may be implied but are subverted, or lack the legal certainty that citizens tend to experience? How are ethnic minorities in Asia transformed from subjects into citizens? What are the duties and obligations of states to accommodate their ethnic minorities as citizens? Under what conditions are ethnic minority rights claims justifiable? How have the post-colonial ideologies of multi-ethnic Asian states, which were often constructed as political entities along arbitrary colonial borders, influenced their conferral of citizenship to ethnic minorities? And how have the philosophies that Asian states and their ethnic minorities attach to citizenship changed over time, and in their interactions with each other?

For the authors of the essays in this special issue, an intellectual inquiry into the nature of the relationship between ethnic minority rights and citizenship is timely and relevant. The strong Southeast Asian geographical focus reflects rapidly unfolding developments in the region that have led to fundamental realignments in the nature of majority-minority relations. The forceful resurgence of ethnic minority grievances in the 1990s was brought about, in the first instance, by the fallout from the 1997 Asian financial crisis, which hit Southeast Asian countries the hardest and triggered the start of national democratization processes across much of the region. These events created multiple fissures and weak points in the authority of national governments in Southeast Asia, which generated space for different viewpoints to be heard, including the voices of marginalized minority groups (Acharya 2003; Miller 2009; Heiduk 2009).

This article canvasses the key issues in this special issue about the practices and structures of inclusion and exclusion of ethnic minorities in contemporary Asian contexts. The approaches to minority issues are highly variegated, encompassing as they do questions pertaining to citizenship, identity and belonging, minority rights, modes and models of accommodation, and human and territorial security. Taken together, however, this collection of essays shares a primary concern with the shifting meanings of citizenship and the rights and responsibilities that such a status confers to ethnic minority populations in rapidly changing Asian societies.

Because of tremendous differences in the localized contextual conditions within and between states in the region, the contributors to this special issue do not propose a 'one size fits all' model for the accommodation of Asia's ethnic minorities. Rather, they explore through theoretical and empirical studies the conditions under which minority accommodation does or does not work, with success being measured by the extent to which ethnic minorities are granted rights and freedoms commensurate to those enjoyed by the ethnic majority population within a given nation-state. The essays assembled in this special issue do not purport to be wholly representative of the viewpoints of the Asian minority stakeholders and ethnic majority groups described herein, and the authors are cognizant of the dangers of casting minorities as homogenous and undifferentiated entities. Recognizing, then, that conversations about minorities normatively take into account individual as well as collective perspectives, this special issue aims to give voice to a range of views for furthering our understanding of how ethnic minorities are positioned in modern Asian societies.

The democratic principle

If there is one unifying principle upon which the contributors to this special issue broadly agree then this is the desirability of forms of minority accommodation modelled on liberal democratic principles. This general consensus mirrors mainstream perspectives among the international community and donor and lending agencies (such as The World Bank, the United Nations Development Programme [UNDP], the International Monetary Fund [IMF], and the Development

Assistance Committee of the Organization for Economic Cooperation and Development [OECD]) which promote rights-based approaches to minority accommodation within a liberal democratic framework. The underlying logic of this approach is that if the rights to freedom of expression and association are central to any meaningful definition of democracy, then it follows that liberal democracies are, or should be, more capable of achieving peaceful and inclusive forms of minority accommodation due to their tendency towards the processes of negotiation and compromise (Miller 2009, p. 7).

Among liberal democrats themselves, however, there is considerable variation in the motivations for supporting rights-based minority accommodation. For the liberal democratic left, the conferral of minority rights is often associated with a process of deepening critical aspects of democratic procedure and good governance, accompanied by the flowering of opportunities for ethnic minorities to constructively engage in state nation-building projects. For the neo-liberal right, granting additional rights and responsibilities to ethnic minorities involves a rolling back of certain state powers in order to rectify failed or failing areas of existing state authority, often via structural adjustment programmes aimed at improving economic efficiency in the provision of community services and public facilities (Crawford and Hartmann 2008, p. 12). Such economic rationalism certainly fuelled the push towards democratization (and in many cases, national decentralization processes) in Southeast Asia following the 1997 Asian financial crisis, especially in Indonesia and the Philippines, and, to a lesser extent, in Thailand. Yet many donors and lending agencies, along with reform-minded civil society actors, also saw the opportunity presented by weakened national governments to strengthen good governance at the local level and reduce social fragmentation by bringing government closer to the people. Such discourses about improving the responsiveness of governments to minority needs and expectations tend to revolve around terms like 'empowerment' and increasing the 'voice' and 'participation' of minorities in public life. In Asia, however, like elsewhere in the world where similar pro-minority projects have taken place, these discourses have often created the illusion of a shared language and common set of priorities when in practice there has been a mismatch between agendas that privilege the subjectivities of the ethnic majority on the one hand, and the aspirations of ethnic minorities on the other hand.

Colonial legacies

The idea of minority accommodation centred on liberal democratic principles has not always been considered desirable by the post-colonial Asian states into which ethnic minorities have found themselves incorporated. Although all of the societies in the states described within this special issue are multi-ethnic in make-up, the circumstances involved in state-formation have tended towards identification with a mono-ethnic national character. Unlike older nation-states in Europe, Asia is awash with states that inherited national borders from former colonial masters in the post-World War Two period of decolonization. Even in Thailand, where no formal colonization took place, the borders of Siam (as Thailand was called until 1939, and from 1945 to 1949) were to some extent determined by independence settlements between British and French colonial powers and the newly independent nation-states of neighbouring Malaysia, Burma/Myanmar, Laos, Vietnam, and Cambodia. The integration of ethnic, religious, cultural, and linguistic minority groups into these reconfigured post-colonial Southeast Asian states was neither a process of natural assimilation nor a clear catalyst for the production of a common national identity. Partly in recognition of this, and partly out of fear of a return to colonial rule, nascent post-colonial governments in the region tended to impose a homogenizing inter-pretation of national identity in a bid to strengthen internal cohesion while confining alternative constructions of belonging to the symbolic realm. These were the same practices that had been used in the past by colonial rulers to manage opposition and contain assertions of difference (Brown 1988, p. 55; Thio 2010, p. 100). Many post-colonial governments in the region also perpetuated, to varying degrees, the racial stereotypes, racialized divisions of labour, and racially demar-cated zones of spatial settlement that had been put in place by the colonial powers before them. These 'colonially constructed commu-nities – and the way in which different "racial" groups were governed in differentiated ways through differentiated spaces' provided a 'taken-for-granted "container" of society' that allowed for the easy reproduc-tion of ethnic or racial distinctions by the dominant ethnic group in the post-colonial era (Bunnell and Coe 2005, pp. 844–5).

The essays in this special issue acknowledge the influence of colonialism in shaping identification to the post-colonial state and nation with the hegemonic ethnic group. In his article, Damien Kingsbury describes how the end of colonial rule in Asian countries rarely resulted in the more equitable realignment of wealth and power relations, fuelling disappointment and disaffection among ethnic minorities. This in turn led weak post-colonial governments to err towards authoritarianism in the channelling of limited state resources to the ethnic majority as a means of retaining control over state institutions, often by nurturing networks of patronage along cultural lines that excluded or suppressed minority voices.

The mono-ethnic character of particular post-colonial Southeast Asian state nation-building projects is illustrated in the country studies in this special issue. In the case of Cambodia, Stefan Ehrentraut shows how ethnic Vietnamese minorities have been marginalized by the racially-exclusionary policies and practices of the Khmer ethnic majority, despite having resided in Cambodia for several generations. Vietnamese immigrants who were once easily incorporated into Cambodia under French colonial rule have been denied citizenship and assigned the status of 'foreign residents' in the post-colonial era. The ongoing disenfranchisement of ethnic Vietnamese in contemporary Cambodia bears testimony to an enduring French colonial legacy in Khmer nationalist circles that plays to local fears of Vietnamese expansionism while reifying a glorious pre-colonial Khmer past. Such mono-ethnic nationalist discourses reinforce the claims to political legitimacy by Khmer ruling elites who portray themselves as protectors of Khmer culture and defenders of Cambodian territorial integrity against insidious forms of 'Vietnameseness'.

As with the Cambodian case, various types of ethnic chauvinism remain alive and well in the state machinery in Thailand. Though Thailand is unique in having retained its absolute monarchy and independence since the thirteenth century, its modern borders were shaped by expansionist colonial powers including French Indochina and British Malaya and Burma. Thailand's centralized system and accusations of 'internal colonialism' by its ethnic minorities can also be traced back to the nineteenth century when Siam negotiated treaties with Western powers and subsequently underwent centralizing structural reforms within a unitary system to consolidate the kingdom's control over its peripheral territories. In his contribution to this special issue, Duncan McCargo explains how Malay Muslims in the southern Thai province of Pattani have sought to physically remove themselves from Thailand via secession following protracted periods of ethnic and racial 'othering' by their fellow Thai Buddhist citizens and state agencies. While Malay Muslims in the south hold formal citizenship, a dominant Thai national identity embodied in the shibboleth 'Nation, Religion, King' has created a strong political culture of opposition to their democratic accommodation at the national level.

For Indonesia and the Philippines, intensive periods of nation-building followed the end of colonial rule in order to strengthen internal unity and manage large populations of indigenous minorities. As Jacques Bertrand explains in his contribution to this special issue, both Indonesia and the Philippines were built out of ethnically-diverse and geographically-dispersed populations that became administratively integrated under colonial rule. While Indonesia's nationalist struggle against the Dutch was waged more spectacularly than the independence revolution (first against the Spanish and then against the Americans) in the Philippines, the nationalist movements in the two countries were at least as much influenced by cooperation with colonialism as by resistance to it (Reid 2004, p. 303). After the formal transfer of sovereignty, however, both fledgling post-colonial states sought to prevent the reassertion of colonial control by adopting models of national integration that institutionally rejected ethnic diversity while symbolically celebrating it. In Indonesia, the state apparatus grew to be dominated by the country's largest indigenous ethnic group, the Javanese, who are also mainly located on the island of Java that is home to the national administrative capital of Jakarta. In the Philippines, too, Muslim indigenous minorities in the south became marginalized by an 'overwhelmingly Christian Philippines state system' (Enloe 1980, pp. 155–6; see also Tuminez 2007, p. 77; Taya 2010).

An unintended consequence of the anti-colonialist movements and subsequent mono-ethnic nation-building projects in the Philippines and Indonesia was the gradual alienation of indigenous minorities from the state. Indigenous minority voices that were silenced for decades under authoritarian post-colonial governments loudly resurfaced in the 1990s with the initiation of national democratization movements and state processes of decentralization. At the heart of indigenous minority demands was the desire for greater autonomy to determine separately those functions that would enable them to protect and maintain their distinctive cultural identity in their own homelands (Clarke 2001; Hirtz 2003; Miller 2004; Rawski and MacDougall 2004).

In his article, Jacques Bertrand focuses on the relatively recent phenomenon of Asian indigenous minority movements in Indonesia and the Philippines to show how these movements have sought to win greater and more equal rights of citizenship based upon culturally specific claims to indigeneity. Bertrand also demonstrates how state forces in Indonesia and the Philippines have attempted to de-emphasize (and to varying degrees delegitimize) the claims to minority rights by indigenous groups in the international arena in order to avoid making strong commitments domestically. While both countries have embraced integrative and inclusive policies in the era of democratic decentralization, such policies have often been framed in the language of ethnic neutrality. Too frequently, notions of 'civic equity' have overlooked the everyday practices of civic exclusion by state institutions that implicitly privilege the ethnic majority. Similarly, inflexible forms of civic citizenship in Indonesia and the Philippines –

along with other countries in the region – have long ignored past injustices against ethnic minorities and the opportunities denied to them through the cultivation of a 'mainstream' national culture that has turned a blind eye to assertions of difference.

Citizenship and belonging

Questions about the desirability of applying Western-derived models of civic citizenship to Asian national contexts are considered by Michelle Miller in her theoretical contribution to this special issue. There is an enduring assumption in Western-dominated citizenship theory that the patterns of citizenship have broadly diverged between Western forms of civic citizenship and an Eastern/Asian trajectory that revolves around ethnic- and racially-based forms of citizenship. Miller explores the internal inconsistencies and inequalities engendered in both civic and ethnic forms of citizenship to argue against the transferability of prescriptive universalizing models of minority accommodation. This is because the idea of a purely civic nation is as fictitious in practice as the ethno-nationalist myths it seeks to dispel and no modern nation-state can be defined wholly in civic or ethnic terms. Furthermore, narrow definitions of civic citizenship may be just as exclusionary of minorities as ethnic forms of citizenship that are built around a shared sense of history and biological lines of descent.

The dangers of relying upon reductionist West–East and civic–ethnic distinctions are highlighted in Gabriele Marranci's essay on the gradations of citizenship and belonging among Muslim minorities in European and Asian national contexts. Focusing on British Pakistani Muslims in the United Kingdom and Malay Muslims in Singapore, Marranci looks at the responses by Muslim minorities themselves to the divergent integration approaches taken by Singapore (which distinguishes Malay Muslims as a separate ethnic, racial, and religious community) and the United Kingdom (where acceptance into the mainstream national culture tends to be predicated upon prior acceptance of 'British values'). In both countries, citizenship is centred on ideas of civic equity and multicultural policies aimed at accommodating multi-ethnic societies. At the same time, the Singaporean system reproduces reductionist 'CMIO' [Chinese-Malay-Indian-Other] ethnic definitional categories that may translate into differentiated life opportunities and social expectations (Leong 1997, p. 85; Barr and Skrbis 2008, p. 51). In the United Kingdom, where integration is individually based and not along community lines, 'Britishness' is often defined by the mass media in opposition to

'Islamic values' (Kundnani 2007; Modood and Ahmad 2007). For British Pakistani Muslims, this othering of Islam in the social sphere fuels feelings of belonging to an 'inferior' minority within an exclusionary mainstream Western culture that sees itself as superior. What Marranci's scholarship shows is that whether in the East or the West, civic citizenship is neither a guarantor of civic equality nor the creation of a meaningful sense of belonging to a political community. Even within nation-states that claim to embrace inclusive and egalitarian forms of citizenship the voices of ethnic minorities can, and often do, tell different stories of exclusion from the margins.

The following essays in this special issue are intellectual interventions into the multi-layered structures and processes of inclusion and exclusion for Asia's ethnic minorities. In particular, the strong geographical focus on Southeast Asian ethnic minorities in this edition is reflective of dramatic regional developments over the past decade in the form of transitions by Southeast Asian national governments away from authoritarianism and towards more democratic forms of accommodation in multi-ethnic societies. These developments have opened up new possibilities for exploring how people who have multiple identities (where identity is primarily associated with a particular ethnicity, region, and/or religion) may be peacefully accommodated if states pursue non-majoritarian, non-plebiscitarian policies that emphasize the protection of both collective and individual minority rights.

The scholars in this special issue do not prescribe a single formula for the accommodation of ethnic minorities in Asia beyond their broad commitment to models of integration and belonging that cohere around liberal democratic principles. Bringing diverse disciplinary perspectives and in-depth knowledge of the region and its peoples, the contributors examine the interplay between multi-ethnic stakeholders and the contextual conditions within which attitudes about identity and belonging manifest, mobilize, and gain or lose ground in the public realm. In sum, these essays provide readers with snapshots of the growing diversity and complexity of ethnic minority issues in Asia and offer insights into the processes and structures through which difference is embraced or subsumed.

In a region as culturally dynamic and diverse as Asia there is much to remind us of the historical imperative of change. Contemporary policies and practices of minority inclusion and exclusion should therefore not be taken as static, enduring, or ends in themselves, but rather as approaches that are in various stages of incompletion and becoming. Within Asia's rapidly changing multi-ethnic landscape, there remains much room for further analysis of what citizenship and minority rights mean in the broader sense of identity and belonging. There is also the need for ongoing revision of current theorizing about ethnic minority issues in order to situate current developments in Asia within broader historical perspectives.

Acknowledgements

I am grateful for the financial and logistical support provided by the Asia Research Institute, National University of Singapore, which made possible the *International Symposium on Ethnic Minorities in Asia*, including the participation of many overseas-based participants. For their exemplary administration of the symposium, I especially thank Alyson Rozells, Valerie Yeo, Sharon Ong, and Henry Kwan. For his valuable editorial support, I am grateful to Sovan Patra. I also wish to thank my favourite critic and life partner, Tim Bunnell, for his thoughtful and stimulating feedback on my own drafts for this special issue.

This special issue is dedicated to Benjamin Donald McKay (13 April 1964 – 18 July 2010), a great scholar, passionate minority rights activist, and dear friend.

References

ACHARYA, AMITAV 2003 'Democratisation and the prospects for participatory regionalism in Southeast Asia', *Third World Quarterly*, vol. 24, no. 2, pp. 375–90

BARR, MICHAEL D. and SKRBIS, ZLATKO 2008 *Constructing Singapore. Elitism, Ethnicity and the Nation-Building Project*, Copenhagen: Nordic Institute of Asian Studies (NIAS) Press

BROWN, DAVID 1988 'From peripheral communities to ethnic nations: separatism in Southeast Asia', *Pacific Affairs*, vol. 61, no. 1, pp. 51–77

BUNNELL, TIM and COE, NEIL M. 2005 'Re-fragmenting the "political": globalization, governmentality and Malaysia's multimedia super corridor', *Political Geography*, vol. 24, pp. 831–49

CLARKE, GERARD 2001 'From ethnocide to ethnodevelopment? Ethnic minorities and indigenous peoples in Southeast Asia', *Third World Quarterly*, vol. 22, issue 3, pp. 413–36

CRAWFORD, GORDON and HARTMANN, CHRISTOFF 2008 'Introduction: decentralisation as a pathway out of poverty and conflict? ', in Gordon Crawford and Christof Hartmann (eds), *Decentralisation in Africa. A Pathway out of Poverty and Conflict?*, Amsterdam: Amsterdam University Press, pp. 7–32

ENLOE, CYNTHIA H. 1980 *Ethnic Soldiers: State Security in Divided Societies*, Athens: University of Georgia Press

HEIDUK, FELIX 2009 'Two sides of the same coin? Separatism and democratization in post-Suharto Indonesia', in Marco Bünte and Andreas Ufen (eds), *Democratization in Post-Suharto Indonesia*, London: Routledge, pp. 295–314

HIRTZ, FRANK 2003 'It takes modern to be traditional: on recognising indigenous cultural communities in the Philippines', *Development and Change*, vol. 34, issue 5, pp. 887–914

KUNDNANI, ARUN 2007 'Integrationism: the politics of anti-Muslim racism', *Race and Class*, vol. 48, no. 4, pp. 24–44

LEONG, LAURENCE WAI-TENG 1997 'Commodifying ethnicity: state and ethnic tourism in Singapore', in Michel Picard and Robert Everett Wood (eds), *Tourism, Ethnicity and the State in Asian and Pacific Societies*, Honolulu: University of Hawai'i Press, pp. 71–98

MILLER, MICHELLE ANN 2004 'The Nanggroe Aceh Darussalam Law: a serious response to Acehnese separatism?', *Asian Ethnicity*, vol. 5, no. 4, pp. 333–51

—— 2009 *Rebellion and Reform in Indonesia. Jakarta's Security and Autonomy Policies in Aceh*, London: Routledge

MODOOD, TARIQ and AHMAD, FAUZIA 2007 'British Muslim perspectives on multiculturalism', *Theory, Culture and Society*, vol. 24, no. 2, pp. 187–213

REID, ANTHONY 2004 'War, peace and the burden of history in Aceh', *Asian Ethnicity*, vol. 5, no. 3, pp. 301–14

RAWSKI, FREDERICK and MACDOUGALL, JOHN 2004 'Regional autonomy and indigenous exclusivism in Bali', *International Journal on Minority and Group Rights*, vol. 11, pp. 143–57

ROBISON, RICHARD 1993 'Indonesia: tensions in state and regime', in Kevin Hewison, Richard Robison and R.odan Garry (eds), *Southeast Asia in the 1990s: Authoritarianism, Democracy and Capitalism*, Sydney: Allen & Unwin, pp. 39–74

SANTAMARIA, M. C. M. 2004 'Framing ethnic conflict and the state in Southeast Asia', *Kasarinlan: Philippine Journal of Third World Studies*, vol. 19, no. 1, pp. 4–36

TAYA, SHAMSUDDIN L. 2010 'The politicization of ethnic sentiments in the Southern Philippines: the case of Bangsamoro', *Journal of Muslim Minority Affairs*, vol. 30, issue 1, pp. 19–34

THIO, LI-ANN 2010 'Constitutional accommodation of the rights of ethnic and religious minorities in plural democracies: lessons and cautionary tales from South-East Asia', *Pace International Law Review*, vol. 22, issue 1, pp. 43–101

TUMINEZ, ASTRID S. 2007 'This land is our land: Moro ancestral domain and its implications for peace and development in the Southern Philippines', *The SAIS Review of International Affairs*, vol. 27, no. 2, pp. 77–91

Post-colonial states, ethnic minorities and separatist conflicts: case studies from Southeast and South Asia

Damien Kingsbury

Abstract

Post-colonial states in the Asian region have frequently been subject to political tensions derived from their multi-ethnic make-up and, what some have argued to be, the failure of states to adequately represent the interests of their ethnic minorities. This article will look at examples of where states in Asia have failed to adequately represent or otherwise incorporate their ethnic minorities as full and equal citizens. It also considers the range of responses to such perceived or actual state failure in adequately incorporating all citizens, including inter-ethnic and racial violence and separatist conflict. The article will conclude by considering conceptual and actual models of state organization intended to resolve racial and ethnic tensions in the Asian region.

Introduction

This paper explores causal elements in claims to separatism in states in Southeast and South Asia. It suggests that each shares some important common elements, key among which is the failure of some post-colonial states to establish citizenship based on a shared sense of civic equity, and a consequent retreat to ethnic specificity. It suggests that a combination of greater civic equity and a higher degree of regional autonomy may address the separatist claims to which it refers.

It has been a common experience that post-colonial states in Asia begin political life, more or less, as united liberal democracies, but quickly slide into disunity and authoritarianism. There have commonly been two processes, often related, by which this has occurred. Post-colonial states, including in Asia, have frequently been subject to political tensions derived from elements of their multi-ethnic or racially-differentiated[1] make-up and what some (although not all) affected minorities have argued to be the failure of states to adequately represent their interests (see Blanton, Mason and Athow 2001 in relation to Africa, and Henderson and Singer 2000 regarding Africa and Asia). In some cases, this political tension has been manifested in claims to a separate political identity, often to a separate state or other form of autonomous polity.

This paper posits three theoretical propositions. The first proposition is that there is a political gap between pre-independence expectations and post-independence realities, which in turn leads to increased competition for scarce resources in multi-ethnic societies encouraging ethnically-specific patron-client relations. A common initial development in newly post-colonial states is that the expectations of liberation from colonialism, including the redistribution of previously expropriated wealth, are rarely met. Indeed, it has been a common experience that not only have post-colonial states not immediately prospered but that they have suddenly lost expertise and access to capital and have materially regressed. The second proposition is that excluded ethnic groups seek redress and, within the context of limited state capacity, governments frequently resort to authoritarian tactics (see, for example, Hirschmann 1987 regarding post-colonial Africa; Cornwell 1999; Englebert 2000; Luis 2000; Feith 2006 regarding the Indonesian experience; also based on the author's regular first-hand observations in Timor-Leste in the period 2002–2006).

Competing for scarce or diminished resources, and within the context of a more, rather than less, authoritarian environment, ethnic groups compete and receive favours on the basis of ethnicity and patronage, with less favoured groups retreating with their grievances to cultural familiarity. Such groups may include those that were historically more separate or self-identifying to the dominant ethnic group/s. Because of a sense of separation (for example, the Acehnese in Indonesia, Southern Muslims in Thailand, Moros in the Philippines), or a sense of compelled inclusion which relegates them to a sense of inferior status (such as the Papuans in Indonesia, Tamils in Sri Lanka, East Timorese in Indonesia, Muslims in Southern Thailand) they have felt marginalized by or alienated from the dominant group. Such grievance and retreat to cultural familiarity around which the group bonds provides the locus of expressions of grievances and protest. Other ethnic groups might feel a lesser degree of separate identity or alienation from the dominant group/s, or may have been able to resolve this sense of separation more positively, in particular through a more active sense of national inclusion or more complete state citizenship.

'Citizenship' is used here to mean the born or naturalized constituent member of a state with equity of rights and duties in relation to that state. Each of the case studies suggests a similar understanding of the principles of 'citizenship', notably relating to 'equity'. However, they can vary in whether the loyalty is to an existing state, a proposed state, or divided between an overarching state and a local autonomous authority.

The third proposition is that political regression involves the political identification around ethnic or tribal groups (vertical distinction, see Smith 1986, p. 87) rather than political identification around group material interests (Grusky, Manwai and Szelenyi 2008; also Shavitt et al. 2006). With the latter, parties tend to form around ideological differences but across the state. With the former, parties tend to form around ethnic familiarity, often geographically specific within the state, and within a system of patron-client relations. Both such political situations have the capacity to challenge basic notions of citizenship, in which, as part of a social contract in which citizens have some responsibilities towards the state, the state and its institutions exist to serve and protect all recognized members of the state equally, if not always with a full complement of rights.

Reacting against the (ethnically majoritarian, authoritarian) state, the state in turn reacts, polarizing politico-ethnic difference. Where such difference has a geographic focus, it may manifest as a specific 'national' identity and a related claim for self-determination based on a new, local claim to a state based on claimed 'just cause' (Mikulas 2006; Buchanan 2007, p. 22).

The qualitative methodology employed here is based on participant observation, primary semi-structured interviews, and discussions with relevant actors in the field over the previous sixteen years. It also draws on related experiences from relevant literature. This paper employs quantitative data only from election outcomes.

In the post-Westphalian era, states have conventionally not accepted the devolution of sovereignty to a separate body and few attempts to secede have been successful. When secession arises states have tended to engage in coercive behaviour, attempting to compel reluctant state members to accept state inclusion. It is this compulsion that some-times engenders rejection. Where it otherwise fails, compulsion generally descends into conflict, in which the dissenting group loses those practical qualities of citizenship upon which the state bases its sovereign claim. This practical loss of the qualities of citizenship, notably equity, apply to the principle case studies of this paper, including Sri Lanka, Thailand, Indonesia, East Timor, and the

Philippines, and the districts or territories within them of, respectively, Eelam, Pattani, Aceh, West Papua, and Mindanao.[2]

These case studies have been chosen because they share a number of similarities: each experience(ed) conflicts in which state boundaries were defined by colonial reach rather than ethnic homogeneity or 'national' identity; they each refer(ed) to claims for ethnic/national separation from the parent state, the groups claiming separation from the state have claimed or continue to claim a separate national identity as a key criterion for their own state, and each separatist group feels or has felt alienated from the state and has claimed state abuses against the ethnic group they claim to represent.

It should be noted that this discussion does not engage in normative, much less dichotomous, debates between 'modernization' and 'tradition'. Rather, it attempts to identify some of the complexities of nationalist claims in multi-ethnic post-colonial states, in turn identifying alternative conceptions of 'nation' and their relative success or failure in maintaining state unity.

Colonial incorporation

When discussing post-colonial states, the arbitrary formation of the colonies upon which they are based raises the question of their artificiality or otherwise, the extent to which they are representative, and whether or not they adequately address the interests of the people whose constituency they claim to represent. Similarly, different political leaders in the region have, at different times, tried to identify what they regard as the qualities of 'good' and 'bad' national membership. To illustrate, the Philippines now holds 'democracy' as a national value (Patino and Velasco 2004), while Indonesia retains its national ideology of *Pancasila* (Five Principles) and defines national membership by acceptance of the military-inspired *Negara Kesatuan Republic Indonesia* (Unitary State of the Republic of Indonesia). In 2009, during its offensive against the Liberation Tigers of Tamil Eelam (LTTE, or Tamil Tigers), the Sri Lankan defence minister justified military retribution against Tamil civilians who had been with LTTE forces on the grounds of their 'disloyalty' (Adams 2009). Similarly, Thailand's Southern Muslims who also hold Malaysian citizenship or speak Malay 'have been persistently accused of disloyalty to the Thai state' (BTI 2008, pp. 4-5; The Nation 2006). Specific ideological requirements associated with such prescriptive loyalty have led to dissent and political tension. This has especially been the case when they have been applied to a uniformity of national identity which has functionally limited pluralism or excluded the participation of ethnic minorities.

Anti-colonialism and national identity

The colonial era in Asia established distinct Westphalian-type borders, which were inherited as a matter of administrative convenience, regardless of ethnic or national make-up, and were the basis for claims to post-colonial statehood. National identity in most states, be it post-colonial or otherwise, tends to cohere around a number of key features, not all of which are necessary but some of which must exist in order for the common bond of mutual political identification to exist. Such features of national identity may include: common language; shared history or myths; common religion or system of beliefs; generally contiguous common territory; and an ethnonym (self-identifying group name) (see Gellner 1983; Smith 1986; Anderson 1991; Connor 1994; Smith 2003). Beyond this, bonds formed of mutual defence sometimes create commonalities which do not otherwise exist (which in turn enhance and contribute to communicability, history/myth, and notions of common territory) (May 2005, p. 1050; Kingsbury 2007, pp. 51–3; see also Erikson 1968). Similarly, such bonds may disappear with the disappearance of the common threat, for example after a colonising power has been displaced.

Critically, however, it appears that nations that do not come to cohere around more sophisticated qualities than an essentialist ethnicity tend to become exclusivist, inwardly focused, and often externally hostile (see Nairn 1981, pp. 347–8). Modern political societies are constituted less around ethnicity or pre-existing 'common characteristics' and more around a common core of civic characteristics, including legal equity, civil and political rights and representative, participatory, transparent, and accountable government. In that these civic characteristics are said to reflect a universal good (if not universal application), an espousal of these is referred to as 'civic cosmopolitanism' or 'civic nationalism'. That is, citizens of a state can transcend ethnic difference and cohere around a sense of civic nationalism, understood as a commitment to common or 'national' identity based on a commitment to core civic principles such as representative and accountable government and equitable rule of law (see O'Donnell and Schmitter 1986, pp. 7-8; Miller 1993; Miller 1995; Smith 1998, pp. 210-13; Kingsbury 2007, pp. 37, 40–2, 56).

Where these features do not exist, where they exist in truncated form, or where they exist separately, e.g., separate language groups with distinct histories in their own contiguous areas, the bonds of mutual political identification will often have not previously existed, are more difficult to establish, and may be predicated upon criteria that is impermanent. To illustrate, culturally-diverse if geographically-proximate peoples who have a common enemy may come together for the purpose of defeating that enemy. The mutual identification around that cause and the social organization required to address it can in itself constitute the basis for the formation of political bonds.

This last point is not only important in the formation of national identity but, in many cases, is central to such identity, not least in the case of struggles for self-determination as exemplified by anti-colonial or post-colonial separatist movements, most of which explicitly identify themselves as 'National' within their titles. This claim to self-determination around the issue of national identity is identified as a 'right' which, under international law, in turn (if in a self-referential manner) legitimizes such a war for self-determination (see Malanczuk 1997). What is important in the claim to national identity is twofold: a) the determination about its status being made by those people in question; and b) the distinction between the idea of 'nation' and the idea of 'state' as conceptual and functional entities which may or may not coincide, and the tensions that might reasonably exist where they do not so coincide. Once that threat has been resolved, the rationale for association can disappear, particularly if there are not significant shared advantages or there are perceived disadvantages in retaining political bonds.

Tensions within post-colonial states

In addition to their relatively arbitrary colonial-era-inspired borders, post-colonial states have been characterized by reduced state capacity following decolonization.[3] In short, the financial and material cost of waging wars of decolonization and the loss of an experienced bureaucracy following decolonization have led to reduced state capacity. In circumstances in which independence from colonialism has often been couched in terms of the material benefits of liberation, the reduction in material welfare of newly-liberated peoples often created new sets of challenges for less experienced post-colonial governments (Henderson and Singer 2000; personal observation in Indonesia 1992–2005, Philippines 1997–2009, and Timor-Leste 2002–2010).

The disappointment and sometimes desperation bred by such material diminution created further sets of tensions. Independence leaders with access to limited state resources have found themselves pressured to buy off key political or ethnic support groups, often in a type of continuation of more traditional patron-client relations (Eisenstadt and Roniger 1980). As a consequence, groups without access to resources or the patronage likely to produce resources were more likely to become alienated from the new state. Where that lack of patronage or alienation was defined along ethnic lines, cleavages arose or were exacerbated. This was especially the case where there had been a colonial-era objection to being incorporated into the colony (for example, Aceh, Pattani, and Mindanao) and reluctance or opposition to being incorporated into the post-colonial state (such as West Papua and Timor-Leste).

Although often drawing on the rhetoric of liberal democracy (or Marxism) as an ideology rationalizing the liberation struggle, when confronted with the combined task of defining the post-colonial state and running it in a reduced capacity, some post-colonial political leaders either implicitly or explicitly drew on interpretations of pre-colonial political traditions, including consensus, respect, and obedience. Faced with dissent from alienated groups, the state can become intolerant, close political space, and functionally lock dissident groups out of state participation. These combined phenomena were present in: Sri Lanka from 1956; Indonesia from 1957, and especially from 1966; in the Philippines notably between 1946 and 1954 and again between 1972 and 1986; and in Timor-Leste increasingly between 2003 and 2006. Where groups were identified by ethnic allegiance, states commonly diminished their practical status as citizens with full and equal legal rights. By way of illustration, East Timorese were targeted by the Indonesian military on a wholesale basis in the period between 1975 and 1978 (Dunn 1996, pp. 275–83), West Papuan resistance leaders have claimed indiscriminate attacks (personal conversations 2005–2009; see also Prai 2000; Grusky, Manwai and Szelenyi 2008), and ethnic Tamils were excluded from much public life due to the 1956 Sinhalese language policy and further claimed they were indiscriminately targeted, especially towards the end of the Eelam war in May 2009 (McDonald 2009). Gerakan Acheh Merdeka (GAM), or Free Aceh Movement, similarly claimed indiscriminate attacks, particularly in the late 1990s.[4]

Group identity

Group identity tends to evolve, as noted, around either ethnic or civic bases. Where civic values, such as a commitment to representative and accountable government and equitable and consistent rule of law, have never been well developed, where they have been weakened, or where they have been systematically disassembled (for example, Indonesia in 1966, Sri Lanka in 2007–2009, Thailand in 2001–2006, and the Philippines in 1972–1986), group identity tends to retreat to that which is common, known, or culturally understood, notably around language, as a bond of social psychology (Kelman 1997; Allott 1998). Within this retreat to the ethnically specific, there are two further broad categories: being ethnically dominant or aggressive (national chauvinism), and ethnically defensive. It is important to note that ethnic group defensiveness does not reflect the opposite of chauvinism or imply a retreat from specific identity, but rather a retreat to and strengthening of that identity as a bond of mutual assurance.

In terms of group response, based on the author's field research,[5] social groups coming from more parochial backgrounds tend to respond in similar ways to external exposure. Such backgrounds can include those that have had no contact with external (including colonial) influences and those that have had limited contact with external influences. This in turn influences how they address issues of social and organizational change, both in relation to themselves and in relation to both dominant groups and subject groups.

In cases where there has been greater positive external exposure, based on personal observation in the field in each of the case studies presented here, it appears there has been a greater tendency to accepting or endorsing cosmopolitan pluralism. This has also been seen in the political rhetoric of a number of anti-colonial and immediate post-colonial political leaders who had been educated in external environments, and among indigenous, pre-modern peoples who have been exposed to more benign external influences, such as multilateral aid organizations. In such cases, there is a greater openness to more fully developed and equitable civic values, for example, among East Timorese who have been educated abroad and among East Timorese who have worked with or been heavily exposed to the UN or aid agencies; among members of the Moro Islamic Liberation Front (MILF) who have negotiated within international forums; within Aceh among the political leadership as well as among many more ordinary Acehnese who had been exposed to international forums and external intervention; among better educated Tamils; and among West Papuans who have been educated or continue to live abroad.[6]

Based on the case studies it appears that the greater the negative external exposure by traditional ethnic groups, the greater the tendency to ethnic specificity or exclusivity. While there are numerous examples of positive exposure, there are significantly more illustrations of the consequences of negative exposure, such as the imposition of arbitrary colonial authority or repression or ethnic or religious majoritarianism. Examples of negative colonial authority or attack apply in each of the case studies, while religious distinction manifested as discrimination can also be said to apply in each of the case studies. Interlocutors from each of the case studies also claimed to have been subject to ethnic majoritarianism.

In circumstances where there is less external exposure, such as in remote parts of Timor-Leste, there is a tendency towards cultural reification, depending on the extent of that exposure. Responses can range from largely ignoring external influences (remote areas of West Papua), constructing them as diminishing and hence reasserting that which is *lulik* ('sacred', Timor-Leste) or reinforcing and further clarifying that which is internal or 'local' as opposed to that which is foreign or external (elements of Aceh, Pattani, and Mindanao).[7] Notably among more isolated ethnic groups such as in Viqueque, Timor-Leste, and more broadly among Sri Lanka's Tamils of the Jaffna Peninsula or the Bangsamoro of Mindanao, when confronted with difference or roused to defence, the more parochial the world view of the inhabitants, the greater the tendency towards conflict with other 'national' groups.

In the case of Viqueque, in Timor-Leste,[8] the period when the people both within Viqueque and Timor-Leste had the highest degree of unity was during the Indonesian occupation, with an imposed external focus enhancing local unity. Similarly, once Sri Lanka's independence was achieved and Tamil's minority status was increasingly contrasted against Sinhalese chauvinism, this quickly led to division and conflict. When Sri Lanka's army commander General Sarath Fonseka said, 'I strongly believe that this country belongs to the Sinhalese' (in Hussain 2009), explaining that ethnic minorities 'can live in this country with us' but could not 'demand undue things', he was imposing an ethnic majoritarian view of national organization. Similarly, Indonesia's Acehnese were active contributors to the war for independence, but quickly became disenchanted with their reduced status following that war, leading to rebellion against the state (see Kell 1995; Reid 2004), while those in West Papua were arbitrarily incorporated into the post-colonial state (Chauvel 2006). 'Even if those making noises number up to a million,' said Indonesia's General Ryzmizard Ryacudu in a familiar majoritarian manner, 'this is a country of more than 220 million people. ... Issues of justice, religion, autonomy, social welfare, education – those are not the Indonesian military's problems' (Emmerson 2005, p. 38).

In other cases, such as the Philippines' Mindanao and Thailand's Pattani, their respective inhabitants were arbitrarily incorporated into the post-colonial state. In the case of Pattani, Siam occupied the sultanate in the late seventeenth century and, following the breakdown of the Siamese state, resumed suzerainty from the mid eighteenth century, creating five new provinces from the one sultanate (Pattani, Narathiwat, Songkhla, Satun, and Yala). However, Pattani had greater commonality with the other Malay Muslim states of the Malay Peninsula. When in 1909 the United Kingdom and Thailand agreed to dissect the Malay Peninsula, Siam was allowed to retain the five provinces created from the Sultanate of Pattani. The residents of Pattani objected, not least because of the subsequent Thai policy of requiring Pattani residents to speak Thai, as well as ascribing Buddhism as the state religion.

The Muslim peoples of Mindanao had similarly lived in independent sultanates, notably Sulu and Maguindanao, until the advent of

Spanish and then American colonialism, to which they refused to concede, having been engaged in a more or less continuous battle against outsiders since the early seventeenth century. The colonial policy of settling Christian Visayans in Mindanao from the early twentieth century further displaced and alienated *katawhang lumad* (indigenous peoples). Mindanao Muslims continue to resist central government authority under various guises, including recently as the Moro[9] National Liberation Front (MNLF), the Moro Islamic Liberation Front (MILF), and Abu Sayyaf Group (ASG). Attempts at reaching peace agreements have been partially successful. Notably, a peace agreement between the government of the Republic of the Philippines and the MNLF in September 1996 unravelled as a result of poor implementation and legislative and executive manipulation, with the agreement formally collapsing in 2001 (May 2002). A subsequent peace agreement with the MILF in 2008 foundered on legal appeal.

Status of case studies

Timor-Leste is arguably the state that has experienced the most extended forms of 'national' division, having first achieved independence from Indonesia in September 1999 and being formally granted independent status in May 2002. Its electoral processes of 1999, 2001, and 2007 have each been marked by an exceptionally high voter turnout[10] and, following near state failure based on politically-manipulated inter-ethnic rivalries in 2006 (number twenty on the Failed State Index 2007, or as a 'failed state', based on 2006 criteria), its elections of 2007 saw democratic change and consolidation, if with a period of post-election violence. In 2008, Timor-Leste began preparing for a programme of decentralization and devolution of political and economic decision-making. This addressed both the limited absorptive capacity of, and economic distribution within, the state, in turn being a key contributor to political tensions, as well as recognizing local political identity.

Aceh had similarly evolved from its status as a reluctant inclusion within the Indonesian state, less completely if perhaps in a more practical manner given its international legal circumstances. Having been a part of the original Republic of Indonesia, Aceh could not claim under international law that it had been illegally occupied after the fact of independence. GAM's political leaders continued to claim that Aceh had participated in Indonesia's war of independence in order to assert its own independence, although a closer reading shows that Aceh's political leadership more accurately wanted a higher level of autonomy within the post-independence state, rather than independence as such. In many respects, the autonomy that GAM agreed to in August 2005, and which was subsequently widely accepted by the

Acehnese people, fulfilled much of the territory's original claims. The creation of local political parties in an otherwise 'national' political party framework allowed for the development of expressions of genuinely local political views, while there was also direct control over a large proportion of the Aceh budget.[11]

In Mindanao, following the earlier peace agreement with the MNLF, the MILF succeeded in winning significant, if yet to be granted, concessions from the central government on an autonomous 'Bangsamoro' (Moro Nation) homeland on 5 August 2008. However, the 'Memorandum of Understanding on Ancestral Domain' (MOA-AD) to create a self-governing autonomous region (MOA-AD 2008) was overturned by the Philippines' Supreme Court on 14 October 2008 on the grounds that it was held to be unconstitutional. The MOA-AD, as the first part of a larger peace agreement including the establishment of a 'juridicial entity', like the 1996 agreement recognized the original self-governing status of the Bangsamoro people and in principle legitimized their political grievances.

The situation for ethnic Tamils in Sri Lanka deteriorated from mid-2006, and in 2009 the Sinhalese-dominated government of President Mahinda Rajapaksa launched a full-scale offensive which, in May 2009, defeated the LTTE. Having failed to militarily win a separate state and refusing to negotiate a compromise agreement,[12] the LTTE's military claim to a separate state was crushed. Having won a military victory and riding a wave of Sinhalese popularity, the Sri Lanka government appeared disinterested in finding a political solution to the ethnic problems that had led to the Tamil's twenty-six year separatist war.

In West Papua, indigenous political leaders continued to oppose both an imposed state of 'special autonomy' and the division of the province into two, Papua Barat and Papua, in 2006, following a failed government attempt to divide the province in three in 2003.[13] A low-level insurgency had been in operation against Indonesian occupation of West Papua since the mid-1960s, following the withdrawal of the Dutch colonial administration in 1962. The territory was formally incorporated into Indonesia via the 1969 'Act of Free Choice', in which 1026 hand-picked tribal chiefs voted in front of armed soldiers to accept integration into Indonesia (Aggelopolous 2009). Over the following forty years, tens of thousands of indigenous West Papuans have been killed and serious human rights violations, along with varying degrees of protest, have continued.[14]

In confronting the Indonesian state, West Papua's indigenous political leadership suffered from division, based on tribal or clan loyalties, degrees of public opposition to Indonesia, and 'big man syndrome'.[15] However, in 2007 the organization of the West Papua National Coalition for Liberation (WPNCL), bringing together most of the separatist organizations (including the armed Free Papua Organization – Organisasi Papua Merdeka, OPM), gave the liberation movement greater coordination and coherence. The Indonesian government, however, responded primarily by ignoring calls for a mediated resolution to West Papua's continuing problems, in turn leaving grievances unaddressed.

Conclusion

In each of the case studies, the ethnic minorities in question had been excluded from equal and consistent rule of law as full state citizens. In part, this exclusion resulted from reactive separatist activity which in turn allowed government agents to construct such ethnic minorities as 'anti-state' and hence beyond the law. However, in each of the case studies, representative groups of the ethnic minorities had questioned or not accepted the extent to which they had been incorporated as full and equal citizens in the first instance, or had been compelled to accept citizenship in ways that were structurally (economically, politically) limiting.

In the case of Timor-Leste, this issue was resolved by the territory achieving independence. In that there remained civic unrest, this was ideological and communal (Kingsbury 2009) and did not represent a separatist claim. In cases where ethnic divisions were problematic, these were largely intended to be addressed by the devolution of state authority to the district level. In Aceh the issue of rule of law as the critical component of an acceptable form of citizenship was addressed by ending the conflict, by limiting the scope and operations of security forces, and by introducing human rights provisions and ensuring rule of law (MOU 2005, pp. 1–2).

In Pattani, separatist conflict, which arose in the late 1940s following the imposition of a particular national identity, was escalated by the abrogation of rule of law under Thailand's Thaksin government. So too in Sri Lanka, Tamils were structurally excluded from participating in the state, including access to rule of law, as a consequence of Sinhalese being made the national language in 1956, even with the ineffective rescinding of that law in 1988. In Mindanao's Muslim regions, rule of law was diminished by relatively arbitrary and religiously-differentiated military violence, which continued to fuel support for separatist claims, while in West Papua, indigenous Melanesians were for the greater part effectively second-class citizens, being subject to rule by law and its sometimes arbitrarily violent interpretation.

In large part, the lack of civic equity reflects a lack of accountability by state institutions to minority groups and conversely it is invariably when there is accountability, via a representative political process, that rule of law has applied. This then raised the prospect of accountable representative political processes providing a source of resolution to ethnic minority claims, presumed in this instance to equate to more or less substantive democracy (Grugel 2006, p. 6), but also accountability. This means the representatives in question actually have to represent their people in a direct sense, to be 'of' them, most directly through proximity an ethnic commonality, or devolved political responsibility. This is especially so if there remains an inherent lack of trust in either the capacity or intentions of central authority.

Finally, the devolution of political authority calls into question the status of the centralized state, and raises the spectre of polities evolving beyond Westphalian and especially centralized sovereignty (see, for example, Ohmae 1995). In part this can be seen to have occurred through the advent and interventions of multilateral institutions such as the UN, the IMF, and the International Criminal Court. In part, too, state sovereignty has been undermined by the 'responsibility to protect' paradigm (UN 2009), and by the acceptance of third-party monitoring in places such as Aceh (EU and ASEAN, 2005–2007), Sri Lanka (Norway, 2002–2007), and Mindanao (Malaysia and Brunei, 2004 to the present).

This article has demonstrated some common features between the case studies. The most critical is the failure of some multi-ethnic post-colonial states to establish citizenship based on a shared sense of civic equity, sometimes caused and usually exacerbated by restricted economic capacity. This failure of the state as an equitable civic institution encourages a retreat to ethnic specificity. It suggests that a combination of greater civic equity, in some cases combined with a higher degree of regional autonomy, may address such separatist claims. As states develop stronger civic institutions, apply the rule of law, and have accountable and representative government, political authority exists primarily to ensure civic welfare, security, and state coordination. Having been born of fragile circumstances, some post-colonial states have thus begun to consider loosening the ties that bind them sometimes too tightly.

Notes

1.   The notion of 'race' is employed here to distinguish physically distinctive peoples, e.g., Papuans and Malays.

2.   Eelam, as referred to by Tamil separatists; and Pattani, the former sultanate, rather than the current province.
3.   This phenomenon is discussed in relation to sub-Saharan African states in John M. Luiz 2000 'The politics of state, society and economy', *International Journal of Social Economics*, vol. 27, no. 3, pp 227-243; Pierre Engelbert 2000 'Pre-colonial institutions, post-colonial states, and economic development in topical Africa', *Political Research Quarterly*, vol. 53, no. 1, pp. 7–36; Richard Cornwall 1999 'The end of the post-colonial state system in Africa?', *African Security Review*, vol. 8, no. 2 ; and David D. Hirschmann 1987 'Early post-colonial bureaucracy as history: the case of the Lesotho Central Planning and Development Office, 1965–1975', *The International Journal of African Historical Studies*, vol. 20, no. 3, pp. 455–70.
4.   Based on personal conversation with the then GAM intelligence coordinator, Irwandi Yusuf in September 2000.
5.   Experience from this field research is cumulative, based on a wide range of experiences variously in remote (mountain village), colonially-acculturated (predominantly urban English, US, Portuguese, or Indonesian educated), and more cosmopolitan (externally educated) communities in Timor-Leste (1995–2010), West Papua (2001–2010), Mindanao (1998–2009), and Sri Lanka (2005–2010).
6.   Based on experience with Acehnese who have been educated or lived abroad, with elements of the leadership of the Free Aceh Movement (Gerakan Acheh Merdeka – GAM), and with Acehnese who have been, as many are, influenced by the flow of ideas from abroad, between 2000 and 2010. Sri Lanka's Tamils were generally better educated by and under the British colonial authorities and continued to privilege education in both the post-colonial state and among its diaspora. Regarding West Papuans, based on experience with West Papuan political leadership between 2001 and 2009.
7.   Regarding Timor-Leste, based on author participant observation, 1995–2010. Regarding Aceh, Pattani, and Mindanao, based on experiences with communities in these environments.
8.   A predominantly Makassae-speaking region.
9.   The term 'Moro' derives from the Spanish word for 'Moors', referring to Muslims who arrived in Spain via Morocco in the early eighth century.
10.   In 1999, 98.5 per cent of registered voters turned out for the ballot for self-determination, with around 93 per cent voting in 2001 and 2007 (taking into account double registration, overseas voters being excluded from the count, and dead voters not being taken off the rolls).
11.   Technically, the provincial government of Aceh controlled 70 per cent of the budget, although in practice this reduced to somewhere between half and two-thirds.
12.   The LTTE claimed that the government's earlier promises to implement political devolution were undermined or not implemented in practice and that it hence had negotiated in bad faith. For its part, senior LTTE strategists (conversation with the author, Kilinochche, May 2006) believed they could expand their claimed homeland, notably to include the major port city of Trincomalee, before negotiating a settlement.
13.   The attempt to divide the province in three was held to be unconstitutional by the Constitutional Court, although the court accepted as *fait accompli* that two provinces had been established.
14.   Despite a number of well-documented massacres, there are no reliable figures on total numbers of deaths. According to Free Papua Organization (OPM) commander Jacon Prai, there have been an accountable 106,000 deaths in West Papua since 1962 (Prai 2000). Budiarjo (2005) claims that 'it is widely agreed that about 100,000 Papuans have lost their lives as a result of military operations or occupation-related disorders since the beginning of Indonesia rule in 1961'. Although Brundige et al. (2004) do not cite a total number of deaths

in West Papua, they do however note that evidence 'strongly suggests' that the Indonesian government has violated the 1948 Convention on Genocide.

15. This is where individuals place most emphasis on their claimed personal or charismatic qualities of leadership rather than constructing and consolidating organizational bases.

References

ADAMS, BRAD 2009 'We cannot ignore Sri Lanka', *Human Rights Watch*, 27 April, New York

AGGELOPOLOUS, NICHOLAS 2009 'Buchtar Tabuni on trial for subversion in West Papua, Indonesia', *Free West Papua*, 22 February, Oxford

ALLOT, ROBIN 1998 'Group identity and national identity', paper presented at conference of *European Sociobiological Society*, Moscow

ANDERSON, BENEDICT 1991 *Imagined Communities*, New York: Verso

BLANTON, ROBERT, MASON, DAVID and ATHOW, BRIAN. 2001 'Colonial style and post-colonial ethnic conflict in Africa', *Journal of Peace Research*, vol. 38, no. 4, pp 473–91

BRUNDIGE, ELIZABETH *et al.* 2004 Indonesian human rights abuses in West Papua: application of the law of genocide to the history of Indonesian control, paper presented to the Indonesian Human Rights Network by the Allard K. Lowenstein International Human Rights Clinic, Yale Law School, April

BTI 2008. *Bertelsman Transformation Index: Thailand 2006*, http://www.bertelsmann-transformation-index.de/126.0.html?&L = 1 (accessed 8 May 2009)

BUCHANAN, ALLEN 2007 'Secession', *Stanford Encyclopedia of Philosophy*, http://plato.stanford.edu/entries/secession/ (accessed 6 May 2009)

BUDIARJO, CARMEL 2005 'West Papua: land of peace or killing field', paper presented to the Fifth International Solidarity Meeting for West Papua, 30 April, Manila

CHAUVEL, RICHARD 2006 *Australia, Indonesia and the Papuan Crises*, Austral Policy Forum 06-14A 27

CONNOR, WALKER 1994 *Ethnonationalism: The Quest for Understanding*, Princeton, NJ: Princeton University Press

CORNWELL, RICHARD 1999 'The end of the post-colonial state system in Africa?', *African Security Review*, vol. 8, no. 2

DUNN, JAMES 1996 *Timor: A People Betrayed*, Sydney: ABC Books

EMMERSON, DONALD 2005 'What is Indonesia', in J. Bresnan (ed.), *Indonesia: The Great Transition*, New York: Rowman and Littlefield

ENGLEBERT, PIERRE 2000 'Pre-colonial institutions, post-colonial states, and economic development in topical Africa', *Political Research Quarterly*, vol. 53, no. 1, pp 7–36

ERIKSON, ERIK 1968 *Identity: Youth and Crisis*, London: Faber & Faber

FAILED STATE INDEX 2007 *Fund for Peace*, http://www.fundforpeace.org/web/index.php?option = com_content&task = view&id = 229&Itemid = 366 (accessed 3 March 2010)

FEITH, HERBERT 2006 *The Decline of Constitutional Democracy in Indonesia*, Jakarta: Equinox [first published in 1962]

GRUGEL, JEAN 2002 *Democratization: A Critical Introduction*, Houndmills: Palgrave

GRUSKY, DAVID, MANWAI, KU and SZELENYI, SZONJA 2008 *Social Stratification: Class, Race and Gender in Sociological Perspective*, Boulder, CO: Westview Press

HENDERSON, ERROL and SINGER, DAVID 2000 'Civil war in the post-colonial world, 1946–92', *Journal of Peace Research*, vol. 37, no. 3, pp. 275–99

HIRSCHMANN, DAVID 1987 'Early post-colonial bureaucracy as history: the case of the Lesotho Central Planning and Development Office, 1965–1975', *The International Journal of African Historical Studies*, vol. 20, no. 3, pp. 455–70

HUSSAIN, IZETH 2009 'Sarath Fonseka and the Sinhalese', *The Island*, http://www.island.lk/2008/11/16/features13.html (accessed 15 June 2009)

KELL, TIM 1995 *The Roots of Acehnese Rebellion 1989–1992*, Cornell Modern Indonesia Project, no. 74, Ithaca, NY: Cornell University

KELMAN, HERBERT 1997 'Nationalism, patriotism, and national identity: social-psychological dimensions', in D. Bar-Tal and E. Staub (eds), *Patriotism in the Life of Individuals and Nations*, Chicago, IL: Nelson-Hall, pp. 165–89

KINGSBURY, DAMIEN 2007 *Political Development*, London: Routledge

——— 2009 *East Timor: The Price of Liberty*, New York: Palgrave

LUIZ, JOHN M. 2000 'The politics of state, society and economy', *International Journal of Social Economics*, vol. 27, no. 3, pp. 227–43

MALANCZUK, PETER 1997 *Akehurt's Modern Introduction to International Law*, New York: Routledge

MAY, RON 2002 'The Moro conflict and the Philippine experience with Muslim autonomy', paper for Centre for Conflict and Post-Conflict Studies, Asia-Pacific Workshop, Canberra

MAY, STEPHEN 2005 'Language policy and minority language rights', in Eli Hinkel (ed.) *Handbook of Research in Second Language Teaching and Learning*, New York: Routledge

MCDONALD, MARK 2009 'Sri Lanka attacks said to kill dozens in hospitals', *The New York Times*, 13 May

MIKULAS, FABRY 2006 'How can we construct a political theory of secession?', paper presented at the annual meeting of the International Studies Association, San Diego, CA, 22 March

MILLER, DON 1993 'In defence of nationality', *Journal of Applied Philosophy*, vol. 10, no. 1, pp. 3–16

——— 1995 *On Nationality*, Oxford: Oxford University Press

MOA-AD 2008 *Memorandum of Agreement on Ancestral Domain*, signed by R. Garca on behalf of the Government of the Republic of the Philippines and M. Iqbal on behalf of the Moro Islamic Liberation Front, Kuala Lumpur, 5 August

MOU 2005 *Memorandum of Understanding Between the Government of Indonesia and the Free Aceh Movement*, Helsinki, 15 August

NAIRN, TOM 1981 *The Break-Up of Britain*, 2nd edn, London: New Left Books

NATION, The 2006 'Raze linguistic, cultural barriers', editorial, *The Nation* 28 June

OHMAE, KENICHI 1995 *The End of the Nation State*, New York: Harper Collins

PATINO, PATRICK and VELASCO, DJORINA 2004 *Election Violence in the Philippines*, Manila: Friedrich Ebert Stiftung

PRAI, JACOB 2000 'An introduction to the genocide', *Irian Jaya (West Papua, New Guinea): The Quest for Independence – April 1 to April 9, 2000*, Kabar Irian, 9 April, http://www.angelfire.com/journal/issues/irian040100.html (accessed 3 March 2010)

REID, ANTHONY 2004 'Indonesia, Aceh and the modern nation state', speech to National Integration and Regionalism in Indonesia and Malaysia conference, University of New South Wales at the Australian Defence Force Academy, Canberra, 26–28 November

SHAVITT, S. *et al.* 2006 'Reflections on the meaning and structure of the horizontal/vertical distinction', *Journal of Consumer Psychology*, vol. 16, no. 4, pp. 357–62

SMITH, ANTHONY 1986 *The Ethnic Origins of Nations*, Oxford: Blackwell Publishers

——— 1998 *Nationalism and Modernism*, London: Routledge

——— 2003 *Chosen Peoples: Sacred Sources of National Identity*, Oxford: Oxford University Press

TAMIL GUARDIAN 2009 'Crackdown on Colombo Tamils', 6 June

WPNCL 2009 'West Papuan leaders call for dialogue with Indonesia', PR-No.7 /2009, Port Vila, 18 June

UNITED NATIONS (UN) 2009 *United Nations General Assembly Resolution 63/308*, New York

Perpetually temporary: citizenship and ethnic Vietnamese in Cambodia

Stefan Ehrentraut

Abstract

There is a clear trend in Western democratic countries towards regularizing the status of long-term ethnic minority residents through the conferral of full and equal citizenship rights. Ethnic minorities who arrived as irregular or temporary migrants in the West are increasingly allowed to follow the immigrant path towards integration into the broader citizenry. This is largely due to recognition that the price of exclusion is not only unjust, but it increases the risk of racial tensions, criminality, and social violence. Investigating the relevance of these Western developments to Cambodia, this article focuses on Cambodia's ethnic Vietnamese minority. Despite residing in Cambodia for generations, ethnic Vietnamese have traditionally been regarded as 'foreign residents' and denied citizenship. Based on extensive field research, this article considers the history and reality of Cambodia's ethnic Vietnamese minority as well as the ethnically-exclusionary policies and practices of the state and Khmer majority towards them.

Introduction

The idea of a distinctly 'liberal' form of multiculturalism has emerged in the West, both in theory and practice, which defends multiculturalism and minority rights as consistent with, and indeed advancing, basic liberal values of individual freedom, democracy, and social justice. One component of this development is a clear trend towards making citizenship available to long-term residents who were previously excluded from it. People who were not thought of as future citizens when they entered a country are increasingly allowed to follow the immigrant path to integration into the larger society. This is in large part due to the recognition that the possible price of exclusion is not only injustice faced by the alienated, ethnically-defined underclass it creates, but also racial tensions, criminality, and violence affecting the larger society and its democratic credentials. Investigating the relevance of these developments for Cambodia, this article analyses contemporary state-minority relationships pertaining to the country's ethnic Vietnamese minority in light of Will Kymlicka's theory of multicultural citizenship. The article explores the considerable histor-ical, legal, political, and social obstacles to ethnic Vietnamese' full membership of mainstream institutions. It is based on extensive field research that was undertaken in 2008 and 2009 and involved interviews and focus group discussions with ethnic Vietnamese, Khmer, and Chinese villagers, community leaders, local government officials, and NGO staff in the provinces of Kratie, Kampong Cham, Kampong Chhnang, Kampot, Kandal, and in Phnom Penh.

Categorizing cultural diversity and minority rights

Kymlicka demonstrates that demands for minority rights and more inclusive citizenship are usefully understood as responses to states' nation-building projects. States engage in deliberate projects of disseminating one national identity among diverse populations, by encouraging and sometimes forcing all citizens to integrate into institutions operating in one national language (2002, p. 343). Different kinds of minorities relate differently to the institutions of aspiring nation-states and respond to nation-building with different strategies and claims. Specifically, it is the mode of minorities' historical incorporation into the state that most profoundly shapes the identities of their members and the relationships with the larger society to which they aspire (Kymlicka 1995, p. 11). National minorities result from the involuntary incorporation into a state of territorially-concentrated, self-governing societies. These groups typi-cally resist the state's nation-building enterprise and seek the perpetuation of their cultures as separate societies alongside the majority culture by claiming self-government and language rights. In contrast, immigrant groups are the result of voluntary decisions by individuals and families to leave their culture and migrate to another country. Typically, immigrant groups do not resist nation-building and do not seek to establish distinct societies within the state. Instead, they aspire to full membership in the larger society and participation in its institutions on a par with members of the majority culture (Kymlicka 1995, pp. 10–26).

The distinction between national minorities and immigrant groups has both descriptive and normative dimensions. Descriptively, it asserts that there are relevant and stable differences between national minorities and immigrant groups in terms of their histories, current characteristics, and future aspirations. Normatively, it suggests that justice in modern states requires group-differentiated citizenship and that differentiation between national minorities and immigrant groups is justified when assigning group-specific rights. Specifically, national minorities are entitled to self-government and language rights while weaker accommodation rights aimed at full membership in the societal institutions of the majority are due to immigrant groups (Kymlicka 2001, p. 91).

A third category of minorities is excluded from membership of mainstream societal institutions, even if their members want to integrate. 'Metics' is what Kymlicka calls this diversely-constituted category of long-term residents who are denied citizenship, such as irregular and temporary migrants, 'guest workers', and refugees. He argues that just nation-building requires that everyone living on the territory must be able to gain citizenship and become an equal member of the nation and that integration is understood in a 'thin' sense, involving primarily institutional and linguistic integration, rather than a 'thick' conception that involves the adoption of particular ways of life (2003, p. 48). In the past, Western democracies responded to the claims of metics with policies of exclusion. However, in the experience of Western countries, it has become clear that those policies have largely failed. Metics who have become *de facto* permanent residents in their new country and who may have established families are unlikely to leave unless they are forced to. Depriving long-term residents of citizenship creates conflicts and tensions that may affect the entire society. It is increasingly recognized that such policies have not only been empirically demonstrated to be flawed but also are normatively inadequate. As Carens puts it, 'human beings who have been raised in a society become members of that society: not recognizing their social membership is cruel and unjust' (2009, p. 3).

Historical incorporation: Vietnamese in Cambodia and Khmer in Vietnam

How have ethnic Vietnamese been incorporated into Cambodia? And, what is the significance of the distinction between national minorities and immigrant groups in Cambodia? The first of these questions can be partly explained by the history of Vietnamese expansionism. From the tenth to the nineteenth century, the Vietnamese state expanded southwards into the kingdom of Champa and further into the Mekong Delta, an area that Cambodia historically considered to be under its jurisdiction and that was previously largely inhabited by communities whose members were ethnically Khmer, though distinct from Cambodia's cultural majority (Chandler 2008, p. 94). This process led to successive waves of Cham migration to Cambodia. What remained of the kingdom of Champa had disintegrated by the middle of the nineteenth century. Vietnamese control over the Mekong Delta was consolidated, and a steady stream of Vietnamese migrated into what is today's Cambodia, dominating the fertile lands along the Mekong River and around the Tonle Sap Lake. Vietnamese expansion culminated in the partial annexation and occupation of Cambodia between 1835 and 1845 by the Vietnamese emperor in Hue, partly in return for Vietnamese protection of Cambodia from Siam. Despite the sharp cultural divide between the two peoples, Cambodia was treated as part of an expanding Vietnam seeking to impose Vietnamese administration, language, and customs (Chandler 2008, pp. 141–61). The removal of large territories from Cambodian jurisdiction, together with the incorporation of a considerable ethnic Khmer population into the Vietnamese state, resulted in a perception of geopolitical insecurity and historical injustice among Cambodians that are among the greatest obstacles to the ethnic Vietnamese' full membership of the Cambodian state today.

The establishment of a French protectorate over Cambodia in 1863 halted the further expansion of the Vietnamese state into Cambodia, but it did not stop Vietnamese immigration. To the contrary, the French encouraged Vietnamese migration to Cambodia, not least to staff their colonial administration (Chandler 2008, p. 185). Ownership of the Mekong Delta remained disputed during the colonial period until it was 'given' by the French to Vietnam in 1947. This decision made permanent the presence of a Vietnamese minority in the Cambodian state and of a substantial ethnic Khmer population in the Vietnamese state. Members of both minorities find themselves on the 'wrong' side of a contested border, but as a result of different modes of incorporation. The Khmer minority in Vietnam was previously a self-governing, territorially-compact Khmer culture that was involuntarily incorporated into Vietnam. Therefore, Western multiculturalism, at least of Kymlicka's persuasion, suggests that the Khmer minority in Vietnam should have the self-government and language rights needed to maintain a distinct society alongside Vietnam's majority culture. In contrast, the incorporation of ethnic Vietnamese into Cambodia was voluntary in so far as there was no coercion on the part of the Cambodian state. Therefore, ethnic Vietnamese in Cambodia are on the immigrant side of the multiculturalist distinction, which suggests that they should have access to citizenship but are not entitled to self-government and language rights.

Ethnic Chinese migrated to, and were integrated into, Cambodia for many centuries and Cham migrants from Champa were more than welcomed by successive Cambodian kings. In contrast, most of the time the Cambodian state neither invited nor encouraged the immigration of ethnic Vietnamese. Ethnic Vietnamese did not historically come with the expectation to integrate into Cambodian society. On the contrary, their coming to Cambodia was linked to Vietnamese as well as French attempts to colonize Cambodia, to integrate Cambodians into an alien culture, and to impose upon them foreign languages and institutions. As the following analysis demonstrates, the historical circumstances of ethnic Vietnamese' incorporation into Cambodia do indeed shape their contemporary relationship with the state and its majority group. Their uncertain citizenship prospects can in part be explained by the way these circumstances differ from those surrounding the incorporation of ethnic Chinese and Cham, as well as from the narratives of immigrants and metics in Western states.

Cambodia's independence and the emergence of the 'Khmer Citizen'

Cambodia achieved independence in 1953. King Sihanouk abdicated in 1955 and became leader of the Sangkum Reastr Niyum (SRN, People's Socialist Community) that dominated the newly-independent state. Sihanouk popularized a new typology of Cambodia's ethnic groups. He classified the diverse hill tribes inhabiting Cambodia's mountainous areas as 'Khmer Loeu' (Highland Khmers), the Cham as 'Khmer Islam', and members of the Khmer minority in the Mekong Delta now belonging to Vietnam as 'Khmer Krom' (Lowland Khmer). These categories continue to be widely used today and shape Cambodian thinking about nation and citizenship. The typology distinguishes between components of the nation but it also implies a distinction between groups that are included (hill tribes, Cham, Khmer Krom) and those that are excluded (ethnic Vietnamese and Chinese). Interestingly, the groups included in Sihanouk's typology are those most plausibly considered national minorities in Kymlicka's classification while the excluded groups are reasonably considered immigrant groups. Arguably, the distinction is the same but the implications are dramatically different. In a liberal multiculturalist framework, both categories of groups are entitled to common citizenship rights while the distinction separates groups with legitimate additional claims to language and self-government rights from those without. In Sihanouk's typology, the same distinction separates citizens from foreigners.

Collins argues that Sihanouk's typology promises 'a pluralist vision of the Cambodian nation' in which 'the minorities of non-Khmer ethnicity' are a permanent feature of the Cambodian nation (Collins 1996, p. 48). This is unconvincing as an official or historical interpretation of Sihanouk's formula, which does not even acknowledge that there are any minorities of non-Khmer ethnicity. Instead, the formula provides a blueprint for a community that is imagined to be homogenously Khmer and in which the only differentiation is topographic and, to a limited extent, religious. This vision is incapable of accommodating national minorities as minority cultures and of integrating members of immigrant groups into the nation. It is compatible with a notion of Cambodian citizenship that includes Cambodia's hill tribes and Cham, but only through their misrecognition, by imposing on them the majority ethnic identity. The typology can be read as a road map for a two-pronged strategy of nation-building that involves the assimilation of hill tribes and Chams and the exclusion of the Vietnamese and Chinese. Much of the suppression of minority identities under Sihanouk – as well as under successive regimes – is consistent with this strategy, which assumes Khmer uniformity where it does not exist and uses the coercive power of the state to impose it on Cambodia's diverse population. Attempts to consolidate a Khmer nation-state based on a thick national Khmer identity are features of all Cambodian regimes since independence. The exclusion of ethnic Vietnamese has been a constant attribute, and indeed a function, of these attempts.

Exclusion of Vietnamese from citizenship during the SRN

A law passed in 1954 formally based citizenship on residence as well as on ethnic descent. The law conferred citizenship on children, at least one of whose parents was Cambodian, as well as on anyone born in Cambodia after 1954 to parents also born in Cambodia: this effectively formalized the exclusion of many ethnic Vietnamese and Chinese (Edwards 1996, p. 119). A naturalization law promulgated in 1954 required five years of residency and 'sufficient' knowledge of the Khmer language but was restricted in 1959 to those with 'sufficient assimilation to the customs, morals and traditions of Cambodia' (Heder and Ledgerwood 1995, p. 22). What is evident in these legal provisions is a strategy of Khmer nation-building that is based on a thick conception of Khmer identity. It was the presence of Vietnamese residents in particular that was the most contested question, and has been since, in how to conceptualize nation and citizenship of the newly-independent state. A National Congress held in 1963 unanimously recommended 'that naturalization be refused in principle to all Vietnamese because they were unassimilateable' and that the citizenship of any naturalized aliens who did not 'respect our traditions' be revoked (Willmott 1967, p. 35). These recommendations are consistent with contemporary policies and practices in that they required prospective citizens to assimilate and adhere to a particular set of traditions. Naturalization is refused to ethnic Vietnamese due to their supposed inability to assimilate into Khmer culture. Of those who are nominally citizens, their legal status and sense of belonging is profoundly insecure because their Cambodian citizenship could be revoked at any time.

Elimination of ethnic Vietnamese from the 'Khmer Race' under the Khmer Republic and Khmer Rouge

Sihanouk was overthrown in 1970 by his cousin, Prince Sirik Matak, and his army chief, Lon Nol, who became president of the 'Khmer Republic'. Lon Nol advocated the superiority of the Khmer race and a violently anti-Vietnamese nationalism. He introduced a new constitutional definition of Cambodians as those who possessed 'Khmer blood, Khmer traditions, Khmer culture, Khmer language and who were born on the territory that is the heritage of our Khmer ancestors' (quoted in Edwards 2007, p. 252). Ethnic Vietnamese residents were not only excluded from citizenship but physically removed from the territory, through pogroms and forceful repatriation. Thousands were massacred, and about 200,000 out of an estimated 450,000 ethnic Vietnamese civilians were forced into South Vietnam (Goshal, Ku and Hawk 1995, p. 20). An estimated 100,000 left in the course of the following five months, before the USA–South Vietnamese invasion of Cambodia in 1970 pushed North Vietnamese forces deeper into Cambodian territories, where they took control of entire provinces. Eventually, these Vietnamese troops defeated Lon Nol's forces and transferred control over those territories to the Khmer Rouge, Cambodia's communist revolutionaries, who took power in 1975.

For all the real revolution the Khmer Rouge brought to Cambodia, the attempt to build a racially-defined Khmer nation by means of expulsion and killing of ethnic Vietnamese closely resembled policies pursued under Lon Nol. As many as 150,000 ethnic Vietnamese were expelled to Vietnam during the first five months of Khmer Rouge rule and most of those who remained were killed (Goshal, Ku and Hawk 1995, p. 21). While all minority identities were violently suppressed in the Khmer Rouge's attempt to build a Khmer nation that coincides with the jealously-guarded borders of the state, only ethnic Vietnamese and, to a lesser extent, the Cham were singled out for systematic exclusion and extinction. Head of state Khieu Samphan declared in 1978 that 'the number one enemy is not US imperialism, but Vietnam, ready to swallow up Cambodia' (quoted in Pouvatchy 1986, p. 447) and the Khmer Rouge attacked Vietnam, with the stated aim of regaining the Mekong Delta. In response, Vietnam occupied Cambodia in 1978, pushed the Khmer Rouge to the border areas and installed a closely-supervised government, the People's Republic of Kampuchea (PRK).

Settling down to a 'normal life' as aliens under the PRK/SOC

During the following years, the Vietnam-supported PRK remained in armed conflict with the anti-Vietnam Coalition Government of Democratic Kampuchea (CGDK), consisting of the Khmer Rouge (now called the Party of Democratic Kampuchea, PDK), FUNCIN-PEC (a royalist party established by Sihanouk), and the republican Khmer People's National Liberation Front (KPNLF). The coalition was united mainly by their shared opposition to the Vietnamese occupation and the 'puppet' PRK government. Most Cambodians were grateful to the Vietnamese for their liberation from the horrors of the Khmer Rouge. But the presence of 100,000 Vietnamese troops as well as Vietnamese technical and political advisers at all levels of the state dominating and 'Vietnamizing' many aspects of Cambodian life was increasingly resented. Due to poverty and repression in Vietnam, the number of ethnic Vietnamese in Cambodia, both former residents and new immigrants, grew to an estimated 300,000 during the 1980s (Chandler 1993, p. 273), which angered many Cambodians. While the PRK leadership was acutely aware of the threat to its nationalist legitimacy posed by the growing number of ethnic Vietnamese residents, they lacked the means to limit immigration and found their Vietnamese masters unresponsive to their concerns (Gottesman 2003, pp. 124–9).

An official policy for ethnic Vietnamese was adopted in 1983, which allowed 'former Vietnamese residents in Kampuchea' to 'quickly settle down to a normal life' (quoted in Goshal, Ku and Hawk 1995, p. 21). Those Vietnamese who had come after the Vietnamese invasion were allowed 'to stay in the country and work', while future immigrants were required to undergo formal immigration procedures. However, the PRK, which changed its name to State of Cambodia (SOC) in 1989, never effectively controlled its borders and most Vietnamese migrants did not bother with formal requirements, although many were able to obtain some form of Cambodian identity papers (Gottesman 2003, p. 163). The PRK/SOC and their supporters considered all ethnic Vietnamese to be foreigners, even those who were formerly Cambodian citizens. By applying to a group of people defined by their ethnicity, PRK/SOC policy reinforced the notion of a separate Vietnamese identity and deprived former Cambodian citizens of Vietnamese ethnicity of their membership status, while entitling an unknown number of Vietnamese citizens to reside and work in Cambodia. PRK/SOC policy was consistent with SRN citizenship in that it normalized the existence of metics, of long-term residents who are excluded from citizenship. PRK/SOC distinctions between different categories of ethnic Vietnamese residents were only temporary, but the distinction between ethnic Vietnamese and other Cambodian residents remained and once again implied the difference between citizens and foreigners.

Contestations of citizenship status within UN peace initiatives

During the Paris peace conference in 1989, attended by Cambodia's political factions and twenty countries, the Khmer Rouge vehemently protested what they claimed were multiple millions of Vietnamese settlers brought in by the Vietnam-controlled PRK in order to take over Cambodia. CGDK parties insisted that all Vietnamese settlers be expelled as part of any political settlement (Heder and Ledgerwood 1995, p. 9). After the collapse of the Paris conference and Vietnam's unilateral withdrawal, CGDK parties continued to insist that Vietnamese troops remained in Cambodia, living among seemingly-civilian ethnic Vietnamese communities. Negotiations at the UN eventually led to the creation of the United Nations Transitional Authority in Cambodia (UNTAC) as part of a peace plan. The prospects of peace, the arrival of tens of thousands of UN personnel, and a subsequent construction boom triggered yet another wave of Vietnamese immigration to Cambodia.

A framework document endorsed by the UN Security Council that had been begrudgingly signed by all Cambodian parties mandated UNTAC with conducting an election with the franchise based on residence. However, when UNTAC drafted the electoral law in 1992, all Cambodian factions, including SOC, strongly protested at the deviation from Cambodia's traditionally ethnicity-based conception of citizenship, specifically the exclusion of ethnic Khmer in Vietnam and the inclusion of ethnic Vietnamese in Cambodia. UNTAC eventually agreed to minor changes designed to reduce the number of eligible voters of Vietnamese ethnicity (Heder and Ledgerwood 1995, p. 24). The following discussion demonstrates that the end of the occupation and the introduction of competitive politics mark the (re-)institutionalization of rhetoric promising to limit or reverse Vietnamese immigration, which has again become an important source of political legitimacy.

Ethnic Vietnamese and the new constitution

The wording of Cambodia's 1993 constitution suggests a return to an ethnicity-based conception of citizenship. Whereas the constitution consistently refers to the country as 'Cambodia', all rights invoked in the constitution are provided to 'Khmer citizens' only. The provision that best captures the ambivalence of 'Khmer citizenship' is in article 31:

> Khmer citizens shall be equal before the law and shall enjoy the same rights, freedoms and duties, regardless of their race, colour, sex, language, beliefs, religion, political tendencies, birth origin, social status, resources or any other position.

The article is open to a range of interpretations, depending on which part is emphasized. Stressing 'Khmer citizens' suggests that citizenship is defined strictly in ethnic terms. Stressing the non-discrimination portion invokes an inclusive conception of membership in a thinly-defined nation. Accordingly, interpretations of this article in literature and public discourse vary widely. One of the most inclusive interpretations claims that it is the 'intention of the constitution to make citizenship available, through the process of naturalization, to persons of Chinese, Vietnamese, and other ancestries' (Clayton 2002, p. 58). This interpretation is implausible given that the constitution does not define citizenship and that it mentions neither minority cultures nor Vietnamese or Chinese, nor even the possibility of naturalization.

In a variation on the same theme, Ovesen and Trankell argue that 'in using the term "Khmer citizen" the Constitution does not imply ethnicity' and that the absence of ethnic minorities from the text of the constitution indicates 'that the nation of Cambodia... no longer needs the kind of nationalism that is based on ethnic affiliation and that people who live and work in their county of birth or chosen residence should be entitled to participate in that country's political affairs' (Ovesen and Trankell 2004, p. 253). But there are virtually no states that people can freely choose as their country of residence and expect to 'be entitled to participation in that country's political affairs'. Even the most liberal-democratic states distinguish between citizens and foreigners and generally let the former participate in political affairs and not the latter. There also is no such thing as nationalism that is entirely free of ethnic affiliation. Any state cannot but operate societal institutions in one language or another, thereby privileging the native speakers of official languages and disadvantaging speakers of others. Ovesen and Trankell's concern with 'discrimination' misses the prior question of citizenship raised by the constitution and by doing so, misconceives the vulnerability of those who reside inside Cambodia but outside the conceptual Cambodian nation.

In contrast to the multiculturalist and civic interpretations of 'Khmer citizenship', Edwards highlights that the constitution, 'taken at its most literal reading, baldly denies basic human rights to anyone so unfortunate as to be labeled non-Khmer' (1995, p. 68). Similar concerns were expressed by various UN institutions and international NGOs. They were validated by Cambodia's National Assembly, whose members agreed during the discussion of the definition of 'Khmer citizen' that it includes hill tribe people and Muslim Cham but not 'people of ethnic Vietnamese origin' (quoted in Amnesty International 1995a, p. 6). Like the SRN conception of citizenship, this definition implies that there can be Khmer citizens of different races, languages, and religions, but it includes hill tribes and Chams only by misrecognizing them as 'Khmer Loeu' and 'Khmer Islam' respectively. At the same time 'Khmer citizenship' excludes 'people of ethnic Vietnamese origin' as a group based on their ethnic identity.

Interestingly, Cambodia's ethnic Chinese were not mentioned in the assembly's discussion. Field research confirms that the problems ethnic Vietnamese face due to their lack of citizenship status are not faced by ethnic Chinese, neither *vis-à-vis* the state nor the general population. Representatives of Cambodia's Chinese community routinely use the term 'Khmer Chen', or 'Chinese Khmer', deliberately invoking and expanding the metaphor used by Sihanouk to include ethnic Chinese into the imagined community of a Cambodian nation defined in Khmer terms. While ethnic Vietnamese remain beyond the realm of 'Khmer' and outside the Cambodian nation, ethnic Chinese have made the transformation from foreigners into citizens, demonstrating the possibility of metics becoming full members of the Cambodian nation.

Immigration and nationality laws: from foreigners to citizens?

A law on immigration was among the first to be sent to the new national assembly in 1994. The law was seen by many as targeting ethnic Vietnamese and constituting the first step toward their deportation (Berman 1996, p. 822). It defines aliens as persons without Khmer nationality but it does not define Khmer nationality, making it impossible to determine reliably who is a Cambodian citizen. All immigrants are required to bring their own passports and to get incoming visas before entering, conditions which most ethnic Vietnamese do not meet. The law requires the deportation and expulsion of aliens who fail to comply with its provisions or who are found to have entered Cambodia illegally. In one reading, the law mandates the mass expulsion of a great proportion of ethnic Vietnamese from Cambodia. Unsurprisingly, the law was met with intense protest from international human rights organizations, from Vietnam, the UNHCR, and even the UN Secretary General. In response, co-Prime Minister Norodom Ranariddh assured the international community that there would be no large scale expulsion of ethnic Vietnamese, and the Ministry of Interior agreed to postpone the implementation of the immigration law until the adoption of the law on nationality (Kirby 1996, p. 33).

The law on nationality, adopted in 1996, does contain a definition of 'Khmer citizen' but it is as ambiguous as earlier legal instruments:

'Any person who has Khmer nationality/citizenship is a Khmer citizen'. As the use of two terms in the English language translation indicates, the respective Khmer term *sancheat* can mean citizenship as well as ethnicity, roughly similar to the English term 'nationality'. Thus the legal definition of 'Khmer citizen' in the nationality law, like the constitution, is compatible with at least two interpretations. In one interpretation, the article states that every Khmer citizen is a Khmer citizen, which has no definitional substance. Alternatively, it means that everyone of Khmer ethnicity is a Khmer citizen, which would exclude all residents who are not ethnically Khmer. The law allows for 'Khmer nationality/citizenship' to be obtained 'regardless of the place of birth' by a child 'who is born from a parent who has Khmer nationality/citizenship', which includes ethnic Khmer in Vietnam. But, given the preceding discussion, there is, clearly, one interpretation that excludes ethnic Vietnamese children, even if they are born in Cambodia. In addition, 'Khmer nationality/citizenship' can be obtained by 'any child who is born from a foreign mother and father who were born and living legally in the Kingdom of Cambodia'. This provision would potentially cover a great proportion of ethnic Vietnamese residents in Cambodia, depending on whether their parents are considered legal residents. But the great majority of Cambodia's ethnic Vietnamese entered Cambodia outside immigration frameworks and therefore, could potentially be considered illegal, even those who were granted Cambodian citizenship under previous regimes.

Naturalization is provided under the law as 'a favor of the Kingdom of Cambodia' and may be 'rejected by a discretionary power'. The favour is linked to the applicant's ability to assimilate into a thick conception of Khmer culture: applicants must speak and read Khmer language, know 'Khmer history', provide 'clear evidence that he/she can live in harmony in Khmer society', and 'get used to good Khmer custom and tradition'. Furthermore, applicants must have lived 'continuously for seven years from the date of reception of a residence card that was issued under the framework of the Law on Immigration'. But no such residence cards had been issued by 2004 (Pyne and Bunly 2004, p. 1) and field research suggests that none have been issued since.

Predictably, the draft law drew strong criticism from various UN institutions and international NGOs. Amnesty International, for example, expressed the concern that 'certain ethnic minorities... may be excluded from nationality rights, and thus be regarded as illegal aliens' (Amnesty International 1995b, p. 63). But the only change to the draft law was the removal of a provision that allowed taking away citizenship from naturalized Cambodians for 'insulting and contemptuous behavior towards the Khmer people'. Interestingly, ethnic Khmer from Vietnam are officially considered Khmer citizens when in Cambodia, which is consistent with the nationality law's definition only if the ethnic interpretation is utilized, which tends to exclude Cambodia's ethnic Vietnamese. Plausibly, the concept of 'Khmer citizen' is meant to serve the double purpose of including ethnic Khmer outside Cambodia and excluding ethnic Vietnamese inside Cambodia.

Field research suggests that a majority of ethnic Vietnamese are not Cambodian citizens, in their own descriptions of their legal status as well as in statements of officials at various levels of the state. However, police authorities frequently issue ID cards in return for bribes. This practice permits unqualified applicants to obtain the appearance of citizenship, while it excludes many who may qualify but lack the money for bribes. The regulation of ethnic Vietnamese residents operates largely outside the legal framework, suggesting that past and current residence is not counted towards the seven years required for naturalization under the nationality law. Ethnic Vietnamese who reside in Cambodia but are not legally citizens face a wide range of legal, political, economic, and social disadvantages. They have no right to vote or to stand in elections, are unable to legally work and own property or to borrow money from banks. They face additional difficulties in accessing social services, in obtaining marriage, birth, and death certificates, building permits, business and driving licences, and in travelling inside and outside Cambodia. Because of their uncertain legal status, ethnic Vietnamese are unable to develop a sense of secure belonging. Their limited access to the legal system reinforces their vulnerability to discrimination and abuse by authorities and the wider society.

Obstacles to ethnic Vietnamese' inclusion: the 'Vietnamese Threat'

There are great similarities between metics in the West and ethnic Vietnamese in Cambodia. Members of both groups were not conceived of as future citizens when they arrived but have made a home in their host country and seek to become full members. As in the West, there is in Cambodia a clear trend towards making citizenship more accessible for metics, but so far it has been limited to ethnic Chinese. Ethnic Vietnamese continue to be considered and treated by state and society as foreigners and outsiders. This difference can in part be explained by the Khmer majority's strong sense of geopolitical insecurity *vis-à-vis* the state of Vietnam. Indeed, the de-securitization of ethnic relations has been a major pre-condition for inclusive citizenship and the adoption of multicultural policies in the West (Kymlicka 2005, p. 34). Western democracies do not generally have neighbours that threaten their territorial sovereignty and their domestic minorities are usually not seen as potential collaborators with hostile powers. In contrast, the exclusion of ethnic Vietnamese from citizenship is seen as justified by Cambodia's security needs, and the inherent right to self-government of a Khmer majority that perceives itself as threatened by the territorial and colonial ambitions of its more powerful neighbour. As Leonard observes, 'the over-whelming nemesis as described by Khmers themselves is Viet-nam...the belief that Vietnam plans to overtake and incorporate numerous provinces of Cambodia is strongly held by Khmers' (Leonard 1996, p. 279).

The idea that Cambodia's existence is threatened by Vietnam is a central myth of nationalist ideology that has been consistently reinforced and perpetuated by political leaders throughout the post-colonial period and across the ideological spectrum (Edwards 1995, p. 56). This is in no small part a legacy of colonialism. By highlighting the past greatness and current smallness of Cambodia and portraying both as stages of a continuous national project, the French projected the Khmer as a people on a trajectory of millennial decline that justified the hegemonic role of the colonialists as Cambodia's saviours from extinction (Barnett 1990). This colonial definition of the Cambodian nation came to be accepted by Cambodian elites and the threat of extinction, typically identified with Vietnameseness, was used by all post-independence regimes to boost their legitimacy as true saviours of the nation (Edwards 2007, pp. 242–56). The perceived risk to the Khmer nation and Cambodian state trumps considerations of justice and democracy that may, otherwise, favour citizenship status for ethnic Vietnamese.

Why ethnic Chinese are citizens and ethnic Vietnamese are not

The perceived threat from Vietnam helps explain why ethnic Chinese today enjoy full and equal citizenship and ethnic Vietnamese do not, even though members of both communities have historically been considered foreigners in Cambodia. There is no shared border with China and no geopolitical risk is perceived to be involved in the historical migration and contemporary residence of ethnic Chinese in Cambodia. Besides, many Cambodians feel that ethnic Vietnamese, by fleeing to Vietnam during the Khmer Rouge years, demonstrated insufficient loyalty to Cambodia or, rather, demonstrated a loyalty to the Vietnamese state inappropriate for Cambodian citizens. This explanation highlights the profound nation-building effect of the Khmer Rouge years, the shared experience of suffering, participation in collectives, and the violent social atomization and assimilation of everyone into a revolutionary Khmer identity monopolized by the Khmer Rouge, an identity that suppressed everyone's culture, beliefs, and traditions. This experience was so universally shared that it made a 'We' that transcends the ethnicity of those who lived through it more possible. It made the Cambodian nation more imaginable as a multiethnic 'We' that fits into a 'Khmer' conception of citizenship. By having shared this experience, ethnic Chinese have come to be part of 'We' while the absence of ethnic Vietnamese reinforced the notion of their separate identity.

Compensation for historical and contemporary injustice

A related difference between metics in the West and ethnic Vietnamese in Cambodia concerns the argument of historical injustice. In the West, long-term residents who have benefitted from more inclusive natur-alization and citizenship policies have tended to be disadvantaged groups at the margins of mainstream society. In contrast, ethnic Vietnamese in Cambodia are perceived to have historically, and unjustly, occupied privileged positions of authority *vis-à-vis* the Khmer majority, as collaborators of Vietnamese and French domination, to which their incorporation before 1975 and their re-incorporation after 1979 are closely linked. In the view of many, the continued exclusion of ethnic Vietnamese compensates for past injustices suffered by Khmers at the hands of the Vietnamese state and for the corroborating role that the ethnic Vietnamese in Cambodia played. The historical injustice argument that supports inclusion in the West thus supports exclusion of ethnic Vietnamese in Cambodia.

Vietnamese control of Cambodia is also invoked as a contemporary argument. In the West, a common justification for the inclusion of metics is that people who are subject to political authority should have a right to participate in determining that authority (Kymlicka 2002, p. 359). By contrast, ethnic Vietnamese in Cambodia continue to be portrayed not only as being outside Cambodian political authority but as helping to subject Cambodians to Hanoi's control. In addition, in the eyes of many Cambodians, the historical and contemporary mistreatment of ethnic Khmers in Vietnam justifies reciprocal unfavourable treatment of ethnic Vietnamese in Cambodia. As Leonard describes a common attitude among the Khmer: 'To sympathize with or to trust Vietnamese at all... is to forget the injustice of taking of Kampuchea Krom lands' (1996, p. 280).

Integration into what? Conceptions of Khmer national identity

A further obstacle to ethnic Vietnamese gaining Cambodian citizen-ship is that the national culture into which citizens are supposed to integrate is thick, in that it is defined, at least nominally, by a specifically Khmer way of life and, sometimes, even as membership of the Khmer race. To many Cambodians, being Cambodian means being Khmer and being Khmer in public discourse is often defined in racial terms (Heder and Ledgerwood 1995, p. 20). As the constitutional concept of 'Khmer citizen' and legal provisions for naturalization suggest, aspirants for Cambodian citizenship are supposed not only to learn the Khmer language, but to become Khmer. Ethnic Vietnamese are not admitted to the nation in part because they are considered incapable of assimilation. However, the fact that Cambodia's ethnic Cham enjoy full citizenship suggests that it is not primarily the degree of assimilation that drives the exclusion of ethnic Vietnamese. Cambodia's Cham energetically maintain a degree of separateness from Khmer mainstream culture that is similar to that of ethnic Vietnamese, although for different reasons. This suggests that the geo-political situation is the decisive factor in determining the possibility of citizenship. With the demise of Champa, Cham ceased to pose a challenge to the Cambodian state and nation. Indeed the Cham and Khmer share a collective narrative of past greatness lost to the Vietnamese state, a commonality that contributes to a sense of 'We' between the two people in which the Vietnamese are essential as the 'other'.

The dynamics of party politics

Other obstacles to ethnic Vietnamese becoming citizens result from the dynamics of party politics. Political parties other than the ruling Cambodian People's Party (CPP), the successor of the PRK/SOC, routinely appeal to strong sentiments against ethnic Vietnamese among the general population for political advantage. A survey undertaken in 2003 found that 30 per cent of the electorate believed that ethnic Vietnamese should not have Cambodian citizenship and should not be allowed to vote. The view that 'the Vietnamese are against Cambodia' was supported by 37 per cent (Asia Foundation 2003, pp. 74–9). One manifestation of this attitude is that Cambodians routinely and publicly use the term 'Yuon' in a derogatory manner to refer to ethnic Vietnamese. Anti-Vietnamese rhetoric feeds on and, thus, is a function of existing fears and prejudices towards ethnic Vietnamese, but the wide use of such rhetoric also reinforces and perpetuates those fears and prejudices. Essential to this rhetoric are claims that the CPP encourages and facilitates large-scale migration of ethnic Vietnamese to Cambodia, that it provides them with Khmer IDs and voting rights, and advances their interest at the expense of Cambodia's, claims that reinforce public support for their exclusion. In the West too, proposals to offer citizenship to metics are contentious but they mobilize citizens on both sides of the issue. In contrast, there are virtually no Cambodian citizens, civil society groups, or politicians advocating on behalf of ethnic Vietnamese to become citizens.

Empirical research suggests that a substantial minority of ethnic Vietnamese vote in Cambodian elections, many with identity cards or family books issued for personal and electoral advantage by local and provincial authorities. These authorities are controlled by the CPP and play essential roles in maintaining election registers. CPP personnel and membership are not necessarily less anti-Vietnamese than other parties but in dealing with ethnic Vietnamese, the CPP is constrained by various agreements with Vietnam as well as demands from the international community. Openly advocating for ethnic Vietnamese or formally improving their legal status would make the CPP vulnerable to claims of insufficient nationalism. The ruling party has no strong interest in ethnic Vietnamese becoming citizens but it does have an interest in them being able to vote. Because all other parties engage in anti-Vietnamese rhetoric, ethnic Vietnamese overwhelmingly vote for the CPP, without the party actually having to respond to their needs. The incentives the ruling party has in this situation help explain why the nationality and immigration laws are not implemented and why identification documents are issued outside the legal framework. The implementation of these laws would necessitate a systematic effort to determine ethnic Vietnamese' family histories and past legal status. It would increase the CPP's vulnerability to charges of being pro-Vietnamese and reveal widespread corruption involved in the sale of Cambodian identification papers over the past decades. It is partly because the ruling party has little to gain from implementing applicable legislation that ethnic Vietnamese' residence and citizenship status remains uncertain and vulnerable to legal challenges. Greater democratization may well lead to the adoption of a more exclusive interpretation of Khmer citizenship and reinforce the marginalization of ethnic Vietnamese. The constitution as well as immigration and nationality laws put few limits to the denial of citizenship rights or even the expulsion of large numbers of ethnic Vietnamese.

Conclusions

Many of the objections to the inclusion of ethnic Vietnamese are based on identifying ethnic Vietnamese with the state of Vietnam, to which most have few links other than their ethnicity. If the two are duly differentiated, inclusion rather than exclusion is the most appropriate response to concerns about the loyalty of Cambodia's ethnic Vietnamese. Citizenship fosters the sense of belonging that strengthens allegiance to Cambodia. In contrast, perpetuating exclusion is more likely to alienate ethnic Vietnamese from Cambodian institutions and to undermine their loyalty to state and society. Making ethnic Vietnamese Khmer citizens not only in legal terms but in terms of language and participation is the most effective way to counter implausible claims that Vietnamese immigration marginalizes Khmers in Cambodia. If the concern is to keep Cambodia culturally Khmer, integration is the most viable and normatively adequate policy option. It would also reduce the considerable potential for ethnic conflict, limit grounds for anti-Vietnamese politics, and shift the political focus to issues that are shared by residents of different ethnicity.

The adoption of a national identity that emphasizes a thin conception of Khmer culture would help advance the idea that ethnic Vietnamese can be loyal and integrated Cambodian citizens. Compared to the violently-exclusive nation-building projects of the recent past, Cambodia has come a long way towards the liberalization of nationalism. In practice, the state is not seen as belonging exclusively to ethnic Khmer but it is, to some extent, shared with other ethnic groups, notably ethnic Cham and Chinese. The adoption of a more open definition of the national community and the possibility of foreigners and even former adversaries becoming citizens is evident in the inclusion of ethnic Chinese and the acceptance of a separate Cham identity. However, Cambodia's ethnic Vietnamese have so far benefitted little from this liberalization.

Among the most important and most politically-feasible measures to improve social inclusion would be to enhance access to public education for children of ethnic Vietnamese parents. This is unlikely to be met by strong objections, since demands for more exclusive policies are often justified precisely on the grounds that ethnic Vietnamese don't speak Khmer. Helping ethnic Vietnamese to learn the Khmer language would reduce objections to inclusion in the longer term. The experience of shared participation in public education is among the most powerful tools of integration and subsequent citizen-making. Claims that ethnic Vietnamese are incapable of integration into Khmer society are implausible in light of the successful integration of ethnic Vietnamese in many countries around the world. Importantly, residents with citizenship prospects have great incentives to make the considerable efforts involved in integration while exclusion and the latent threat of deportation undermine such incentives.

Effective integration requires the implementation of legislation related to immigration and nationality. This should be done with a view to regularizing the legal status of ethnic Vietnamese. There is a need to distinguish between citizens and immigrants. Long-term ethnic Vietnamese residents who do not qualify for citizenship should be issued residence cards under the framework of the immigration law, which would put them on a path to citizenship. In many cases, the determination of legal status will depend on who is given the benefit of the doubt. To avoid statelessness and reduce the number of residents with insecure and irregular legal status, it should be given to law-abiding ethnic Vietnamese. It should be recognized that in many cases the original terms of admission have become irrelevant. Determining the legal status of a child born to ethnic Vietnamese parents today based on whether or not its grandparents entered Cambodia within an immigration framework that may have existed on paper only is neither feasible nor justifiable. Ethnic Vietnamese who have lived for many years in Cambodia, and in many cases were born there, are *de facto* members of Cambodian society. They should be legally recognized as such.

Given that many Cambodian citizens oppose naturalizing ethnic Vietnamese, it would be prudent to regulate more thoroughly and possibly limit future immigration. This would reduce the perception that recent, temporary, or future immigrants benefit indiscriminately from the inclusion of those who qualify under relevant laws. It would also reduce the plausibility of anxieties about large numbers of future settlers flooding Cambodia and help create a transparent and predictable process that is trusted by citizens, encourages integration of immigrants, and contributes to an inclusive and just conception of Cambodian citizenship. However, it would be unrealistic to expect this to happen as long as the rule of law remains absent and impunity and corruption prevail in Cambodia.

Acknowledgements

Field research was undertaken by Chen Sochoeun and the author and supported by the Heinrich Böll Foundation. I am grateful to Thida Heidinger and Chen Sochoeun as well as my reviewers for helpful comments on earlier drafts of this article. Remaining mistakes are mine.

References

AMNESTY INTERNATIONAL 1995a *Cambodia: Human Rights and the New Government*, London: Amnesty International
—— 1995b *Cambodia: Diminishing Respect for Human Rights*, London: Amnesty International
ASIA FOUNDATION 2003 *Democracy in Cambodia – 2003: A Survey of the Cambodian Electorate*, Phnom Penh: Asia Foundation
BARNETT, ANTHONY 1990 'Cambodia will never disappear', *New Left Review*, no. 180 March–April, pp. 101–25
BERMAN, JENNIFER S. 1996 'No place like home: anti-Vietnamese discrimination and nationality in Cambodia', *California Law Review*, vol. 84, no. 3, pp. 817–74
CARENS, JOSEPH H. 2009 'The case for amnesty: time erodes the state's right to deport', *Boston Review*, May/June, p. 4–14
CHANDLER, DAVID 1993 *A History of Cambodia*, Chiang Mai: Silkworm Books
—— 2008 *A History of Cambodia*, 4th edn, Boulder, CO: Westview Press
CLAYTON, THOMAS 2002 'Language choice in a nation under transition: the struggle between English and French in Cambodia', *Language Policy*, vol. 1, no. 1, pp. 3–25

COLLINS, WILLIAM 1996 'The Chams of Cambodia', *Interdisciplinary Research on Ethnic Groups in Cambodia*, final draft reports, Phnom Penh: Center for Advanced Study

EDWARDS, PENNY 1995 'Imaging the other in Cambodian nationalist discourse before and during the UNTAC period', in Heder, Steve R. and Judy Ledgerwood (eds), *Propaganda, Politics, and Violence in Cambodia. A Democratic Transition under United Nations Peace-Keeping*, New York: M. E. Sharpe

—— 1996 'Ethnic Chinese in Cambodia', *Interdisciplinary Research on Ethnic Groups in Cambodia*, final draft reports, Phnom Penh: Center for Advanced Study

—— 2007 *Cambodge: the Cultivation of a Nation, 1860–1945*, Honolulu, HI: University of Hawai'i Press

GOSHAL, BADAS, KU, JAE H. and HAWK, DAVID R. 1995 *Minorities in Cambodia*, London: Minority Rights Group

GOTTESMAN, EVAN 2003 *Cambodia After the Khmer Rouge: Inside the Politics of Nation Building*, New Haven, CT: Yale University Press

HEDER, STEVE R. and LEDGERWOOD, JUDY 1995 'Politics of violence: an introduction', in Steve R. Heder and Judy Ledgerwood (eds), *Propaganda, Politics, and Violence in Cambodia. A Democratic Transition under United Nations Peace-Keeping*, New York: M. E. Sharpe

KIRBY, MICHAEL 1996 'Report of the Special Representative of the Secretary-General for Human Rights in Cambodia', UN Economic and Social Council

KYMLICKA, WILL 1995 *Multicultural citizenship: A Liberal Theory of Minority Rights*, Oxford: Oxford University Press

—— 2001 *Politics in the Vernacular: Nationalism, Multiculturalism, and Citizenship*, Oxford: Oxford University Press

—— 2002 *Contemporary Political Philosophy: An Introduction*, Oxford: Oxford University Press

—— 2003 'Western political theory and ethnic relations in Eastern Europe', in Will Kymlicka & Magdalena Opalski (eds), *Can Liberal Pluralism be Exported?: Western Political Theory and Ethnic Relations in Eastern Europe*, Oxford: Oxford University Press

—— 2005 'Liberal multiculturalism: Western models, global trends, and Asian debates', in Will Kymlicka and Baogang He (eds), *Multiculturalism in Asia*, Oxford: Oxford University Press

LEONARD, CHRISTINE S. 1996 'Becoming Cambodian. Ethnic identity and the Vietnamese in Kampuchea', *Interdisciplinary Research on Ethnic Groups in Cambodia*, final draft reports, Phnom Penh: Center for Advanced Studies

OVESEN, JAN and TRANKELL, ING-BRITT T. 2004 'Foreigners and honorary Khmers: ethnic minorities in Cambodia', in Christopher R. Duncan (ed.), *Civilizing the Margins. Southeast Asian Government Policies for the Development of Minorities*, Ithaca, NY: Cornell University Press

POUVATCHY, JOSEPH R. 1986 'Cambodian-Vietnamese relations', *Asian Survey*, vol. 26, no. 4, pp. 440–51

PYNE, SOLANA and BUNLY, NHEM CHEA 2004 'Laboring illegally. Officials flexible in enforcing aspects of immigration law', *Cambodia Daily*, Phnom Penh, January 24–25, p. 3

WILLMOTT, WILLIAM E. 1967 *The Chinese in Cambodia*, Vancouver: Publications Centre, University of British Columbia

Why scholars of minority rights in Asia should recognize the limits of Western models

Michelle Ann Miller

Abstract

This article considers the relationship between ethnic and racial minority rights and citizenship in Asia. The most ethnically divided and populous region in the world, Asia is home to some of the most contrasting state responses to ethnic minority assertions of diversity and difference. Asia is also awash with wide-ranging claims by geographically-dispersed ethnic minorities to full and equal citizenship. In exploring the relationship between ethnic minority rights claims and citizenship in Asia, this article considers the relevance of certain core assumptions in Western-dominated citizenship theory to Asian experiences. The aim is to look beyond absolutist West–East and civic–ethnic bifurcations to consider more constructive questions about what Asian and Western models might learn from one another in approaching minority citizenship issues.

Introduction

In a world where there is increasing awareness of ethnic diversity, ethnic minorities are becoming more, rather than less, demographically numerous.[1] Tensions between minority and majority populations are on the upsurge as states struggle to absorb indigenous and immigrant ethnic minority groups into their processes of nation-building. Occupying a prominent place on the global map of ethnic and racial conflict, Asia is marked by significant linguistic, cultural, religious, political, social, and economic cleavages and territorial disputes. The region is also characterized by some of the most divergent state responses to ethnic conflict, ranging from violent military repression and coercion on the one hand, to various offers of autonomy and other forms of self-rule aimed at granting ethnic minorities more equal citizenship on the other. Similarly, Asia's ethnic minorities have responded to state nation-building projects in varying ways, ranging from peaceful accommodation, to subordination to the state's homogenizing tendencies, to the adoption of a competing nationalist ideology, to the pursuit of economic rights as a means of circumventing political inequalities engendered in state-defined citizenship.

This article considers some theoretical dimensions of the relationship between ethnic minority rights and citizenship in Asia. This relationship is complex and varied, but in general, recent theorizing has tended to focus either on the contested legitimacy of ethnic minority rights claims to citizenship (e.g., Pakulski 1997; Bauböck et al. 2006; Cowan 2008; Verkuyten 2008) or the value and meaning of citizenship as the primary unit of analysis (such as Connover, Searing and Crewe 2004; Wray-Lake, Syvertsen and Flanagan 2008; Brewer 2009; Fortier 2010). In the former category, proponents of ethnic minority rights typically fall into one of three camps: 1) human rights advocates who argue that ethnic minorities are inherently disadvantaged and that their rights must be protected against the hegemony of the majority population; 2) those who seek to protect minority groups against ethnic dilution in an increasingly multicultural and globalized world; and 3) minority political actors who claim ethnicity or race as the basis for their discrimination against, or assertion of power over, the ethnic majority. By contrast, detractors of ethnic minority calls for more inclusive citizenship tend to endorse a uniform majoritarian order with an inflexible understanding of difference, or contend that privileging minority rights claims based on ethnicity risks impairing the state's effectiveness to rule in other areas.

In the second category, there is broad consensus that the criteria for citizenship are neither static nor enduring, and that the meaning of citizenship has varied considerably over time (Jenson 1997; Joppke 2007; Dalton 2008; Colombo 2010). Yet despite this acceptance of the fluidity and differentiated patterns of citizenship, there is an enduring assumption in Western-dominated citizenship theory that the trajectories of national development have fundamentally diverged between Western civic citizenship and an Eastern/Asian model that primarily conceives of citizenship in ethnic and racial terms. The corollary of this assumption with regard to ethnic minority rights is that Western liberal democratic models of civic citizenship grant minorities equal and inclusive citizenship irrespective of their race or ethnic background, whereas Asia's ethnic minorities are often portrayed as marginalized 'subjects' who lack the same rights and legal certainty that the status of 'citizen' confers to the ethnic majority.

In exploring the relationship between ethnic minority rights claims and citizenship in Asia, this article seeks to clarify some of the misconceptions associated with this core assumption in Western-dominated citizenship theory while considering its relevance to Asian experiences. The aim is to look beyond absolutist West–East and civic–ethnic bifurcations to consider more constructive questions about what Asian and Western models might learn from one another in conceptualizing the relationship between citizenship and Asia's ethnic minorities. In this, it is important to note the dangers of obscuring variations in geographically-dispersed conflicts between ethnic minorities and majority populations over the nature and content of citizenship, which are individually unique and distinct. All ethnic minorities have particular localized conditions and circum-stances that must be taken into account in navigating their relationship with nationality and citizenship. In so far as the following pages draw parallels between 'Western' and 'Eastern'/'Asian' discourses on citizen-ship, then, it is with a view to assessing the relevance of some assumptions in Western-dominated citizenship theory about minority rights in Asia. The aim is not to present a model of 'Asian citizenship' as an equally narrow response to Western citizenship theory, but rather to consider the potential of Asia as an empirically-rich laboratory for theorizing about minority rights and citizenship, both in an intra-Asia context as well as in terms of the region's contribution to the ever-growing body of citizenship theory more broadly.

Subjects or citizens?

First, let us consider the sometimes paradoxical distinction between subjects and citizens. In its simplest sense, a 'subject' is one who is governed over by a monarch or other ruler (Moon and Davidson 1995, pp. 1-2). In this unequal power relationship the rights of the subject are limited to the prerogatives of the ruler, who is not necessarily bound by any reciprocal obligation to protect the welfare of his/her subjects in return for their service and subordination. By contrast, the term 'citizen' as it derives from the Greek civic republican city-state, the *polis*, or the Latin *civis* (Pocock 1998, p. 31), infers a measure of equal membership of the state, including a formal set of rights, responsibilities, and practices that define and reinforce this constituent membership.[2] As a modern ideal, citizenship is also associated with a moral equivalence for all citizens through their shared commitment to social justice principles and through the equalizing of opportunities in order to manage differences between citizens (Young 1989, p. 250).

For practical purposes, however, the distinction between subjects and citizens is not always so neatly delineated. Subjects are not instantly transformed into citizens as citizenship rights tend to be obtained gradually, often through protracted struggle. As Cruikshank points out, 'citizens are not born; they are made' (1999, p. 3) through what she calls the 'technologies of citizenship', or the skills, knowledge, programmes, and other tools aimed at empowering people to constructively engage as citizens (Cruikshank 1999, p. 1). During this process of making (or unmaking) citizenship, there may be confusion over whether groups and individuals are subjects or citizens, or both. For instance, history is replete with examples of colonial subjects who have enjoyed many of the same rights and freedoms as their colonial masters without ever having had those rights constitutionally enshrined. Even a former colonial power like Great Britain has been the site of considerable uncertainty over the rights of British citizens in relation to their subject status before the Crown.[3] There have also been debates in Britain and in other liberal democracies over the extent to which the broad bundle of rights and entitlements that are generally associated with citizenship in such a system are undermined or subverted by the contingencies of a given period. For example, participation theorists would argue that a dominant government and weakened opposition in a parliamentary democracy where argument and debate are reduced to a largely perfunctory role tend to produce an electorate that comprises cynically-disengaged subjects rather than citizens (Wright 1994, p. 27).

Such ambiguities over the distinction between subject status and citizenship are especially prevalent in cases involving ethnic minorities. All states struggle to manage ethnic diversity and difference, not only amongst their own citizens, but also between citizens and non-citizens. Most, if not all, states fail to establish ethno-culturally neutral public institutions, which privilege the subjectivities of the majority population in a multitude of ways (Pholsena 2005, pp. 80-1). Although Western European and North American models of citizenship have strived towards more egalitarian and inclusive forms of national membership since the mid-twentieth century after a period of massive reversals in citizenship (for example, in Germany's Third Reich from 1933 to 1945, and under the White Australia policy from 1901 to 1973), indigenous and migrant ethnic minorities in the West have continued to decry their real or perceived treatment as 'second class' citizens. Across much of Asia, too, attempts to establish more inclusive frameworks for citizenship following democratization in the late 1990s have been destabilized by clashes between forcefully-resurgent minority groups and majority populations over the rights and entitlements of citizenship. This has been very much the case with India's ethnic minorities in Jammu and Kashmir and the northeast region, with Muslim minorities in the southern Philippines, and in Indonesia with Papuans, and until recently, the Acehnese and the East Timorese.

East–West citizenship dichotomies

The persistence of tensions and conflicts between ethnic minorities and majority populations has spawned a vast body of literature on minority rights claims to citizenship. This literature originated in the West and has been dominated by Western academics to include a strong normative commitment to the liberal democratic principles of equality, liberty, and social justice. It has also been frequently coupled with an *a priori* assumption about the universal applicability 'of the practices and supporting justifications of the trajectory of citizenship in the West', including the implicit or explicit idea that people who do not live in liberal democracies should 'become more like us' (Heisler 2005, p. 669). Yet while Western theories of citizenship have travelled to influence many parts of Asia, they have usually only been partially applied in relation to minority rights, or have met with accusations of moral imperialism and arrogance by post-colonial states against their former colonial masters. Of course, such arguments have been advanced by Asian governments to promote culturally-relativist ideologies and to justify repressive policies toward ethnic minorities while delegitimizing their claims to more equal rights and entitlements. However, to dismiss the critics of Western citizenship theory so lightly would be to overlook the numerous internal contradictions between this idealized universal rights regime and the 'inequalities engendered by market competition, race, and immigration' (Ong 1999, p. 263). It would also be to ignore certain 'horrors perpetrated on the road to the ideas and ideals of citizenship that might be offered for export' (Heisler 2005, p. 669) by the West, including its history of slavery, physical elimination (by mass expulsion or genocide) of indigenous minorities, coercive assimilation of immigrants, and active political exclusion of women and the poor. Moreover, non-Western multi-ethnic societies have their own traditions for peacefully accommodating minorities (He and Kymlicka 2005, p. 1), just as all the major religious traditions – Confucianism, Buddhism, Hinduism, Christianity, Judaism, and Islam – have belief systems for conceptualizing and practising the tolerance of difference in diversity.

Civic versus ethnic citizenship

One of the key assumptions in Western citizenship theory about the relationship between minority rights and citizenship in Asia pertains to the foundational myth of nationalism. There is an enduring acceptance that Western liberal democratic trajectories of citizenship have departed from the East through their coherence around a core set of consciously chosen civic principles, or civic nationalism. Set in opposition to this is the idea that national membership in many parts of Eastern Europe, the Middle East and Asia is defined by the ethno-nationalist myth of a shared identity based around a common culture and ancestry. This myth is perpetuated by at least four sources. First, it is reinforced by scholars who seek to understand and make sense of national identity and belonging in contemporary Asian contexts through an historical lens of ethnicity, often emphasizing the importance of indigenous ethnic struggles against Western colonial rulers in the processes of post-colonial nation-building (see, for example, Wessel 1994; Ahmed 1998; Phadnis and Ganguly 2001; MacKerras 2003; Brown 2005; Snitwongse and Thompson 2005). Second, the myth of common ancestry is perpetuated by sections of ethnic majority populations in Asian countries, especially in cases where there is a high degree of ethnic homogeneity such as in Japan, Korea, and China (Karmel 2002; Shin 2006; Doak 2008). It is also found in multi-ethnic Asian states where one ethnic group predominates: for instance, in Indonesia the Acehnese, Papuans and other aggrieved ethnic minorities have accused the numerically dominant ethnic Javanese of Dutch-style 'internal colonization' and of cultural domination via formal transmigration policies (see, for example, Chauvel and Bhakti 2004; Davies 2006; Miller 2009). Third, myths of shared history and biological lines of descent are manufactured by Asia's numerous ethno-nationalist minority movements (and their supporters), who argue for greater autonomy or physical separation from their parent states by reifying (and to varying degrees reinventing) claims to a separate and distinct pre-colonial history.[4] For example, such ethno-nationalist myths are perpetuated by minorities in India's northeast and Jammu and Kashmir regions, by Malay Muslims in southern Thailand, by Muslim minorities in the southern Philippines and by various minorities such as the Kachin, Karen, and Shan ethnic groups in Burma/Myanmar. Fourth, absolutist ideologies such as the 'Asian values thesis' which ascribes distinctive 'non-Western' or 'pan-Asian' categories to Asians in their relationship with the state as citizens perpetuates the myth of differential values and belief systems for different peoples along racial lines (Tarulevicz 2008, p. 140).

While it is true that Asia has experienced patterns of ethnic integration differently from the West – which complicates the interplay between civic and ethnic elements in (especially post-colonial) nationalist discourses – the logic of employing such distinctions between Western-civic and Eastern-ethnic nationalism and citizenship is problematic, both in relation to ethnic minority rights issues and more generally. Most obviously, such heuristics cannot be mapped onto 'Asia' as a whole without subscribing to reductionist 'Asian values' style arguments about Asia as a coherent and unified entity. Beyond this, in the real world a pure civic nation is as mythical as the ethno-nationalist myths it seeks to dispel (Yack 1996). As Yack (1996),

Kymlicka (2001, p. 24), Smith (1991, p. 13), and others point out, no modern nation-state defines citizenship in civic or ethnic terms alone, just as all forms of nationalism comprise civic and ethnic elements, which predominate alternately at particular junctures in history. There is also a 'large gray zone' of policies and practices that could fit into either category, such as requiring immigrants to learn the language of the ethnic majority, which may either 'be seen as reinforcing an ethnic sense of nationhood or as promoting civic participation in the political process' (Brubaker 2004, pp. 139-40). Furthermore, as Yack points out, it is mistaken to assume that civic identity is tied to rational choice and voluntary political membership whereas ethnic identity is hereditary and emotionally based, because civic identity is often inherited too (1996, pp. 196-7).

The coupling of an East–West dichotomy with the civic–ethnic divide is equally problematic since, like many other such parallels, it tends to produce simplistic and misleading stereotypes. Stephen Shulman, who directly challenged this dual dichotomy in his 2001 survey of fifteen countries about attitudes towards the criteria for national identity and membership, found that the 'civic-West/ethnic-East stereotype, when true, is only weakly true, and according to several measures is false' (2002, p. 554). Notwithstanding the obvious limitations of measuring attitudes about nationhood and citizenship in aggregate terms, which Shulman himself acknowledges, the survey revealed that whereas 'most of the West has a long tradition of democracy and relatively strong and stable political institutions, cultural conceptions of nationhood are alive and well, and support for multiculturalism is relatively weak' (Shulman 2002, p. 583). Furthermore, though states in the West have generally sought to accommodate their ethnic minorities through policies of multiculturalism, such attitudes have not been strongly reflected among the wider populace, thereby raising broader questions about the extent to which states are capable of shaping national identities as well as the attitudes and practices of ordinary citizens.

Another problem with civic-ethnic reductionism in relation to minority rights claims is the assumption that the civic nation is inherently 'good', rational, and inclusive whereas the ethnic nation is 'bad', emotive, and exclusionary of ethnic minorities (see, for example, Ignatieff 1993; Breton 1988, pp.86-7; Heater 2004; Brown 2007; Ipperciel and Woo 2009, pp. 169-70). Implicit in this viewpoint, as championed most ardently by North American political theorists, is the idea that civic and territorial conceptions of the nation are superior to the ethnic nation with its 'focus on the genealogy of its members, however fictive; on popular mobilization of "the folk"; on native history and customs; and on the vernacular culture' that seeks to recreate an imagined community of ancestral *ethnie* (Smith 1993, p. 5).

In other words, the liberal, 'neutral' civic nation as a bonded 'community of equal, rights-bearing citizens' (Ignatieff 1993, pp. 6–7) is seen to offer more egalitarian and inclusive forms of citizenship than the illiberal and racially-biased ethnic nation, which characterizes ethnic minorities as genealogically different and therefore inferior to the majority population. The perils of ethnic nationalism are quite legitimately emphasized in many cases where nationalist ideologies have been employed to repress ethnic minorities. But such criticisms are rarely levelled against civic nationalism, which has also been responsible for the exclusion of ethnic minorities in myriad ways. Many multi-ethnic states have sought to impart a sense of civic solidarity through the production and imposition of 'a myth of [ethnic] homogeneity' (Thorpe 2007, p. 90). Such homogenization is typically created by adopting a narrow definition of civic citizenship that focuses on state patriotism, and through policies of assimilation that deny legitimacy to pre-existing ethnic and cultural identities while manufacturing new forms of civic national identity. This myopic production of civic citizenship is especially common during wartime (Neufeldt 2009) and often occurs via mass education programs (Montefiore 2005, p. 98). Over recent years in Western 'civic' countries, the limits of toleration for ethnic diversity by majority populations have been shown through the categorization by governments of 'Muslim immigrants as a cultural problem, spawning courses designed to alter immigrants' beliefs and practices in the name of civic integration' (Bloemraad, Korteweg and Yurdakul 2008, p. 159). A variation of this theme relates to the prohibition from the public realm of cultural and religious traditions that are important to ethnic minorities, such as the ban in France of Muslim girls from wearing headscarves in state schools. In Asia, too, fears of multiple ethnic loyalties vying for primary loyalty to the nation-state have produced exclusionary citizenships and the denial of ethnic and cultural allegiances outside structures sanctioned by the state. This has been shown in Sri Lanka in its brutal treatment of the Tamil minority, in Cambodia with the Vietnamese minority, and with southern Thailand's ethnic Malay Muslim minority, to name but a few examples. Undemocratic governments across Asia have also manufactured and perpetuated a homogenizing nationalist agenda to legitimize their continued rule. This happened in Indonesia under the New Order regime (1966–1998), which legitimized authoritarian rule through the institutionalization of its nation-building project; this was so effective that the contradictions between belonging to an ethnic minority and being Indonesian became a largely post-New Order phenomenon because 'the trajectory of maturation, taking one through the schools especially, left one "Indonesian"' (Siegal 2000, p. 366). Through this imposition of a narrow sense of what it meant to be 'Indonesian', the

Indonesian state succeeded, until recently, in suppressing ethnic assertions of diversity and difference or in confining them to the symbolic realm within institutional niches controlled by the state (Miller 2009, pp. 43-4).

Despite the many problems engendered in the civic–ethnic bipolar configuration, it does retain some value in conceptualizing ethnic minority rights claims to citizenship. The value of this distinction lies in understanding how ethnic minorities may be protected from injustices perpetrated in the name of 'civic' and 'ethnic' integration alike, as well as the conditions under which ethnic minority rights claims are made and justified. The East–West bifurcation, while itself highly problematic on a number of levels (see, for example, Lieberman 1997; Brennan 2001), can nonetheless provide a useful conceptual tool for identifying broad differences in the historical trajectories of nation-building. In the West, patterns of national development have moved away from a narrow emphasis on duties and responsibilities to the state and towards a greater emphasis on the rights of groups and individuals, including those of minorities. Of course, Western models are not entirely inclusive or neutral; Western liberal democracies place numerous demands on minorities in that they tend only to be committed to ethnic diversity up to the point that the equal rights of ethnic minorities do not infringe upon those of the ethnic majority, like most other systems. There are also a host of lingering problems that make ethnic minorities in Western liberal democracies feel like less than equal citizens, including ignorance, indifference, or resentment towards minorities by the majority population and the persistence of old homogenizing nation-state rhetoric and practices (Kymlicka 2005, p. 115). Even so, by all accounts Western liberal democracies have enjoyed a high degree of success in accommodating ethnic minorities and have largely succeeded in normalizing the expectation that minorities are entitled to at least the same rights as the majority population, and sometimes to additional group-differentiated rights and entitlements.[5]

Little wonder, then, that in Asia's pluralistic societies Western ideas about multiculturalism and minority rights have gained increasing credence in dealing with ethnic conflicts. These ideas have been transmitted to the region via a number of channels. Western-educated Asian elites returning to their own countries have made a significant impact upon legislative debates and government policy choices about ethnic minority issues (Delanty and He 2008, p. 334). International donor and lending agencies have also played a big role in shaping Asian government and civil society attitudes about liberal democratic models of citizenship and minority rights by prescribing policy advice in exchange for financial disbursements. Growing democratization in Asia, too, has produced new systems and political leaders who have looked beyond a 'military solution' to their ethnic conflicts and towards new forms of peaceful accommodation within nascent democratizing regimes (Miller 2009, pp. 184-5).

In light of the influence, broadly wielded, by the Western liberal democratic paradigm, it is curious that countries in Asia have tackled similar sorts of ethnic and racial minority issues using starkly divergent techniques. Whereas the Philippines has been relatively successful in integrating its indigenous ethnic minorities (Malanes 2002; Gatmaytan 2007), Indonesia has been less accommodating of native minority groups on indigenous grounds (Li 2000; Persoon 2004). But Indonesia has been significantly innovative in handling its armed ethno-nationalist conflict in Aceh by granting the Acehnese people meaningful self-government within the Indonesian state, and in dealing with the East Timor dispute through its decision, in 1999, to grant the East Timorese people a referendum on national self-determination. By contrast, the Philippines, Thailand, Sri Lanka, Burma/Myanmar, and other countries in the region have continued to rely heavily on a traditional security approach in their handling of ethnic minority disputes. In dealing with non-violent ethnic tensions, Asian states have also differed tremendously. In Malaysia, for example, there is an ethnically-based political system that is meant to accommodate ethnic minority viewpoints, and yet it reinforces an unequal hierarchy led by ethnic Malay 'sons of the soil' while constitutionally marginalizing non-Malay citizens (Endicott and Dentan 2008; Bunnell, Najarajan and Willford 2010). Across the border, Singapore's meritocratic system embraces multiculturalism and emphasizes the equality of all citizens while at the same time reproducing essentialized 'CMIO' (Chinese-Malay-Indian-Other) ethnic definitional categories that may translate into differentiated life opportunities and expectations in the social sphere (Barr and Skrbis 2008, p. 51; Tarulevicz 2008).

What these cases point to is the extensive diversity in citizenship experiences and civic attitudes that underpin approaches to minority rights in Asian national contexts. While Western liberal democracies continue to be marked by differentiated citizenships that distinguish the 'haves' from the 'have nots' (Hajnal 2007, p. 560; Vázquez-Arroyo 2008, p. 127), the gradations of inclusion and exclusion are far more subtle and varied in Asia. Unlike Western liberal democracies, where a basic set of rights and entitlements are attached to formal notions of citizenship (such as rights to freedom of thought, speech and religion, rights to vote in elections and to apply for a passport), in many Asian countries the boundaries between formal and informal rights are often blurred, or lack the legal certainty that is typically associated with citizenship in the West (for instance, when legislation discriminates against citizens belonging to a particular ethnic group, or when social institutions limit rights accommodation). Whereas violent ethnic and racial conflict is a now a rarity in the West, clashes between ethnic minorities and majority populations over state borders also remain commonplace in Asia. Unlike most Western liberal democracies, Asia is strewn with multiethnic societies that inherited national borders from their colonial masters in the recent post-Second World War period of decolonization. This has led to the incorporation of heterogeneous indigenous minorities whose pre-existing loyalties and identities have not always sat comfortably alongside the nation-building projects of post-colonial states. Many states in Asia have dealt with these assertions of ethnic diversity and difference by employing the same or similar tactics to those once used in the West, such as the repression or elimination of indigenous ethnic minorities, the adoption of racially-based entry policies for immigrants and the forced assimilation of ethnic minorities into the hegemonic majority population (Santamaria 2004, p. 7; Thio 2010, p. 100). Yet some Asian countries have come to view ethnic minorities not as a problem to be annihilated or forcibly assimilated, but rather as groups and individuals who can play a constructive role in the processes of national development rather than in opposition to it (Duncan 2008, p. xvi; Miller 2009, pp. 165-6).

The adoption of Western liberal democratic frameworks for citizenship in parts of Asia should not be interpreted as meaning that Western models necessarily represent the ideal response to ethnic minority rights claims. Whether in the East or the West, states employ policies that comprise inclusive as well as exclusionary elements. Equally, just as no state defines citizenship in entirely civic or ethnic terms, both categorizations may be employed to empower *or* marginalize ethnic minorities in a multitude of ways. The multi-layered domains of citizenship cannot be easily encapsulated by 'West–East' and 'civic–ethnic' bifurcations. Cross-cutting flows of knowledge and exchange between the West and Asia continually throw into question many of the underlying assumptions about civic virtue in the governance of citizenship. That is, assumptions about civic virtue tend to be normative representations of civic engagement in public life that only exist in partial and incomplete forms in the everyday management and practices of citizenship. Rather than adopting such narrow dichotomies of conceptualization then, the nature of the relationship between ethnic minority rights claims and citizenship in Asia could be approached more constructively by considering how the conferral of ethnic minority rights can work to strengthen rather than weaken the bonds of civic solidarity. In this, inclusive forms of civic solidarity would place less emphasis on state patriotism and the reproduction of a common national identity than on the various modes of belonging to a political community to accommodate the diversity of its members.

Notes

1.   Studies of ethnic minority populations are typically conducted at the national level, where census data reflects a trend towards growing ethnic minority populations. For broader studies of this trend see, for example, David Coleman 2009 'Divergent patterns in the ethnic transformation of societies', *Population and Development Review*, vol. 35, no. 3, pp. 449–78; Commission of the European Communities 2006 *The Demographic Future of Europe – From Challenge to Opportunity*, Brussels: Commission Communication; David Coleman 2004 'Partner choice and the growth of ethnic minority populations', *Bevolking en Gezin*, vol. 33, no. 3, pp. 7–34.

2.   Whereas membership of the Latin *civitas*, or the community of citizens, entailed 'modes of legal relations that established themselves between members' under civil law, non-citizens were subject to other forms of authority or engaged in simple power struggles. For more in-depth analysis of the historical relationship between citizens and non-citizens, see, for example, Paul Magnette and Katya Long 2005, *Citizenship: The History of an Idea*, Colchester: European Consortium for Political Research (ECPR) Press, p. 7.

3.   For an in-depth analysis of this debate see Christopher Vincenzi 1998 *Crown Powers, Subjects and Citizens*, London: Continuum International Publishing Group, pp. 90-1.

4.   Unlike older nation-states in the West, the great majority of Asian countries were established less than one century ago by preserving borders set by former colonial administrators that artificially divided 'a large culture area into several sovereign states' (Smith 1981, pp. 136–7).

5.   For a useful overview of the competing merits of universal versus group-differentiated rights in Western citizenship theory, see, for example, Tim Bunnell 2008 'Multiculturalism's regeneration: celebrating *Merdeka* (Malaysian independence) in a European Capital of Culture', *Transactions of the Institute of British Geographers*, vol. 33, no. 2, pp. 254–7.

References

AHMED, ISHTIAQ 1998 *State, Nation and Ethnicity in Contemporary South Asia*, London: Pinter

BARR, MICHAEL D. and SKRBIS, ZLATKO 2008 *Constructing Singapore. Elitism, Ethnicity and the Nation-Building Project*, Copenhagen: Nordic Institute of Asian Studies (NIAS) Press

BAUBÖCK, RAINER, KRALER, ALBERT, MARTINIELLO, MARCO and PERCHINIG, BERNHARD 2006 'Migrants' citizenship: legal status, rights and political participation', in Rinus Penninx, Maria Berger and Karen Kraal (eds), *The Dynamics of International Migration and Settlement in Europe*, Amsterdam: Amsterdam University Press

BLOEMRAAD, IRENE, KORTEWEG, ANNA and YURDAKUL, GOKCE 2008 'Citizenship and immigration: multiculturalism, assimilation, and challenges to the nation-state', *Annual Review of Sociology*, vol. 34, pp. 153–79

BRENNAN, TIM 2001 'The cuts of language: the East/West of North/South', *Public Culture*, vol. 13, no. 1, pp. 39–63

BRETON, RAYMOND 1988 'From ethnic to civic nationalism: English Canada and Quebec', *Ethnic and Racial Studies*, vol. 11, no. 1, pp. 85–102

BREWER, MARILYNN B. 2009 'Social identity and citizenship in a pluralistic society', in Eugene Borgida, Christopher M. Federico and John L. Sullivan (eds), *The Political Psychology of Democratic Citizenship*, Oxford: Oxford University Press, pp. 153–75

BROWN, DAVID 2007 'Ethnic conflict and civic nationalism: a model', in James L. Peacock, Patricia M. Thornton and Patrick B. Inman (eds), *Identity Matters. Ethnic and Sectarian Conflict*, Oxford: Berghahn Books, pp. 15–33

——— 2005 *The State and Ethnic Politics in Southeast Asia*, London: Routledge [1st edn, London: Routledge, 1993]

BUNNELL, TIMOTHY 2008 'Multiculturalism's regeneration: celebrating *Merdeka* (Malaysian independence) in a European Capital of Culture', *Transactions of the Institute of British Geographers*, vol. 33, no. 2, pp. 251–67

BUNNELL, TIM, NAJARAJAN, S. and ANDREW WILLFORD 2010 'From the margins to centre stage: "Indian" demonstration effects in Malaysia's political landscape', *Urban Studies*, vol. 47, no. 6, pp. 1257–78

CHAUVEL, RICHARD and BHAKTI, IKRAR NUSA 2004 *The Papua Conflict: Jakarta's Perceptions and Policies*, Washington, DC: East–West Centre

COLEMAN, DAVID 2009 "Divergent patterns in the ethnic transformation of societies", *Population and Development Review*, vol. 35, no. 3, pp. 449–78

—— 2004 'Partner choice and the growth of ethnic minority populations', *Bevolking en Gezin*, vol. 33, no. 3, pp. 7–34

COLOMBO, ENZO 2010 'Changing citizenship: everyday representations of membership, belonging and identification among Italian senior secondary students', *Italian Journal of Sociology of Education*, vol. 4, no. 1, pp. 129–53

COMMISSION OF THE EUROPEAN COMMUNITIES 2006 *The Demographic Future of Europe – From Challenge to Opportunity*, Brussels: Commission Communication

CONNOVER, PAMELA JOHNSTON, SEARING, DONALD D. and CREWE, IVOR 2004 'The elusive idea of equal citizenship: political theory and political psychology in the United States and Great Britain', *Journal of Politics*, vol. 66, no. 4, pp. 1036-68

COWAN, JANE K. 2008 'Culture and rights after Culture and Rights', *American Anthropologist*, vol. 108, issue 1, pp. 9–24

CRUIKSHANK, BARBARA 1999 *The Will to Empower: Democratic Citizens and other Subjects*, Ithaca, NY: Cornell University Press

DALTON, RUSSELL J. 2008 'Citizenship norms and the expansion of political participation', *Political Studies*, vol. 56, no. 1, pp. 76–98

DAVIES, MATTHEW N. 2006 *Indonesia's War over Aceh. Last Stand on Mecca's Porch*, London: Routledge

DELANTY, GERARD and HE, BAOGANG 2008 'Cosmopolitan perspectives and Asian transnationalism', *International Sociology*, vol. 23, no. 3, pp. 323–44

DOAK, KEVIN M. 'Narrating China, ordering East Asia: discourse on nation and ethnicity in Imperial Japan', *Journal of the Washington Institute of China Studies*, vol. 3, no. 1, pp. 1–24

DUNCAN, CHRISTOPHER R. 2008 'Introduction. Advances and setbacks: ethnic minority rights and resources (2004–2007)', in Christopher R. Duncan (ed.), *Civilizing the Margins. Southeast Asian Government Policies for the Development of Minorities*, Singapore: National University of Singapore Press, pp. ix–xx

ENDICOTT, KIRK and DENTAN, ROBERT KNOX 2008 'Into the mainstream or into the backwater? Malaysian assimilation of Orang Asli', in Christopher R. Duncan (ed.), *Civilizing the Margins. Southeast Asian Government Policies for the Development of Minorities*, Singapore: National University of Singapore Press, pp. 24–55

FORTIER, ANNE-MARIE 2010 'Proximity by design? Affective citizenship and the management of unease', *Citizenship Studies*, vol. 14, issue 1, pp. 17–30

GATMAYTAN, AUGUSTO (ed.) 2007 *Negotiating Autonomy. Case Studies on the Philippine Indigenous Peoples' Land Rights*, IWGIA Document 114, Quezon City: International Working Group on Indigenous Affairs

HAJNAL, ZOLTAN L. 2007 'Black class exceptionalism: insights from direct democracy on the race versus class debate', *Public Opinion Quarterly*, vol. 71, no. 4, pp. 560–87

HE, BAOGANG and KYMLICKA, WILL 2005 'Introduction', in Will Kymlicka and Baogang He (eds), *Multiculturalism in Asia*, New York: Oxford University Press, pp. 1–21

HEATER, DEREK 2004 *Citizenship. The Civic Ideal in World History, Politics and Education*, Manchester: Manchester University Press [1st edn, Harlow: Longman, 1990]

HEISLER, MARTIN O. 2005 'Introduction – changing citizenship theory and practice: comparative perspectives in a democratic framework', *PS: Political Science & Politics*, vol. 38, issue 4, pp. 667–71

IGNATIEFF, MICHAEL 1993 *Blood and Belonging: Journeys into the New Nationalism*, New York: Farrar, Strauss & Giroux

IPPERCIEL, DONALD and WOO, JENNIFER 2009 'Between freedom and belonging: Ignatieff and Berlin on nationalism', *British Journal of Canadian Studies*, vol. 22, no. 2, pp. 155–75

JENSON, JANE 1997 'Fated to live in interesting times: Canada's changing citizenship regimes', *Canadian Journal of Political Science*, vol. 30, no. 4, pp. 627–44

JOPPKE, CHRISTIAN 2007 'Transformation of citizenship: status, rights, identity', *Citizenship Studies*, vol. 11, issue 1, pp. 37–48

KARMEL, SOLOMON M. 2002 'Ethnic nationalism in mainland China', in Michael Leifer (ed.), *Asian Nationalism*, London: Routledge, pp. 38–62 [1st edn, London: Routledge, 2000]

KYMLICKA, WILL 2005 'Models of multicultural citizenship: comparing Asia and the West', in Sor-hoon Tan (ed.), *Challenging Citizenship. Group Membership and Cultural Identity in a Global Age*, Aldershot: Ashgate Publishing Limited, pp. 110–36

———— 2001 *Politics in the Vernacular. Nationalism, Multiculturalism and Citizenship*, Oxford: Oxford University Press

———— 1996 *Multicultural Citizenship*, Oxford: Oxford University Press

LI, TANIA MURRAY 2000 'Articulating indigenous identity in Indonesia: resource politics and the tribal slot', *Comparative Studies in Society and History*, vol. 42, no. 1, pp. 149–79

LIEBERMAN, VICTOR 1997 'Transcending East–West dichotomies: state and culture formation in six ostensibly disparate areas', *Modern Asian Studies*, vol. 31, issue 3, pp. 463–546

MACKERRAS, COLIN (ed.) 2003 *Ethnicity in Asia*, London: RoutledgeCurzon

MAGNETTE, PAUL and LONG, KATYA 2005 *Citizenship: The History of an Idea*, Colchester: European Consortium for Political Research (ECPR) Press

MALANES, MAURICE 2002 *Power from the Mountains. Indigenous Knowledge Systems and Practices in Ancestral Domain Management. The Experience of the Kankanaey-Bago People in Bakun, Benguet Province, Philippines*, International Labour Organization INDISCO Case Study no. 8, Baguio City Toplinq

MILLER, MICHELLE ANN 2009 *Rebellion and Reform in Indonesia. Jakarta's Security and Autonomy Policies in Aceh*, London: Routledge

MONTEFIORE, ALAN 2005 'Liberalism, identity, minority rights', in Sor-hoon Tan (ed.), *Challenging Citizenship. Group Membership and Cultural Identity in a Global Age*, Aldershot: Ashgate Publishing Limited, pp. 98–109

MOON, MICHAEL and DAVIDSON, CATHY N. 1995 'Introduction', in Michael Moon and Cathy N. Davidson (eds), *Subjects & Citizens. Nation, Race, and Gender from Oroonko to Anita Hill,* Durham, NC: Duke University Press, pp. 1–8

NEUFELDT, REINA C. 2009 'Tolerant exclusion: expanding constricted narratives of wartime ethnic and civic nationalism', *Nations and Nationalism*, vol. 15, issue 2, pp. 206–26

ONG, AIHWA 1999 'Cultural citizenship as subject making: immigrants negotiate racial and cultural boundaries in the United States', in Rodolfo D. Torres, Louis F. Miron and Jonathan Xavier Inda (eds), *Race, Identity and Citizenship. A Reader*, Oxford: Wiley-Blackwell Publishing, pp. 262–94

PAKULSKI, JAN 1997 'Cultural citizenship', *Citizenship Studies*, vol. 1, issue, 1, pp. 73–86

PERSOON, GERARD A. 2004 'Indonesia: reformulating indigenous identity', *IIAS (International Institute for Asian Studies) Newsletter*, no. 35, p. 11

PHADNIS, URMILA and GANGULY, RAJAT 2001 *Ethnicity and Nation-Building in South Asia*, New Delhi: Sage Publications [1st edn, New Delhi: Sage Publications India Pvt Ltd, 1989]

PHOLSENA, VATTHANA 2005 'A liberal theory of minority rights for an illiberal multi-ethnic state?', in Will Kymlicka and Baogang He (eds), *Multiculturalism in Asia*, New York: Oxford University Press, pp. 80–109

POCOCK, J. G. A. 1998 'The ideal of citizenship since classical times', in Gershon Shafir (ed.), *The Citizenship Debates*, Minnesota, MN: University of Minnesota Press, pp. 31–42

SANTAMARIA, M. C. M. 2004 'Framing ethnic conflict and the state in Southeast Asia', *Kasarinlan: Philippine Journal of Third World Studies*, vol. 19, no. 1, pp. 4–36

SHIN, GI-WOOK 2006 *Ethnic Nationalism in Korea: Genealogy, Politics and Legacy*, Stanford, CA: Stanford University Press

SHULMAN, STEPHEN 2002 'Challenging the civic/ethnic and West/East dichotomies in the study of nationalism', *Comparative Political Studies*, vol. 35, no. 5, pp. 554–85

SIEGAL, JAMES T. 2000 *The Rope of God*, 2nd edn, Ann Arbor, MI: University of Michigan Press

SMITH, ANTHONY D. 1981 *The Ethnic Revival in the Modern World*, Cambridge: Cambridge University Press

—— 1991 *National Identity, Reno*, NV: University of Nevada Press

—— 1993 'The ethnic sources of nationalism', *Survival*, vol. 35, no. 1, pp. 48–62

SNITWONGSE, KUSUMA and THOMPSON, W. SCOTT (eds) 2005 *Ethnic Conflicts in Southeast Asia*, Singapore: Institute of Southeast Asia (ISEAS) Publications

TARULEVICZ, NICOLE 2008 'Hidden in plain view: Singapore's race and ethnic policies', in Nicholas Tarling and Edmund Terence Gomez (eds), *The State, Development and Identity in Multi-Ethnic Societies. Ethnicity, Equity and the Nation*, London: Routledge

THIO, LI-ANN 2010 'Constitutional accommodation of the rights of ethnic and religious minorities in plural democracies: lessons and cautionary tales from South-East Asia', *Pace International Law Review*, vol. 22, issue 1, pp. 43–101

THORPE, JULIE 2007 'Belonging in Austria: citizens, minorities and refugees in the twentieth century', in Matt Killingworth (ed.) *Europe: New Voices, New Perspectives. Proceedings from the Contemporary Europe Research Centre Postgraduate Conference 2005/2006*, Melbourne: Contemporary Europe Research Centre, pp. 90–104

VERKUYTEN, MAYKEL 2008 'Support for multiculturalism and minority rights: the role of national identification and out-group threat', *Social Justice Research*, vol. 22, no. 1, pp. 31–52

VINCENZI, CHRISTOPHER 1998 *Crown Powers, Subjects and Citizens*, London: Continuum International Publishing Group

WESSEL, INGRID (ed.) 1994 *Nationalism and Ethnicity in Southeast Asia*, Munster: LIT

WRAY-LAKE, LAURA, SYVERTSEN, AMY K. and FLANAGAN, CONSTANCE A. 2008 'Contested citizenship and social exclusion: adolescent Arab American immigrants' views of the social contract', *Applied Developmental Science*, vol. 12, issue 2, pp. 84–92

WRIGHT, TONY 1994 *Citizens and Subjects: An Article on British Politics*, London: Routledge

YACK, BERNARD 1996 'The myth of the civic nation', *Critical Review*, vol. 10, issue 2, pp. 193–211

YOUNG, IRIS MARION 1989 'Polity and group difference: a critique of the ideal of universal citizenship', *Ethics*, vol. 99, no. 2, pp. 250–74

Integration, minorities and the rhetoric of civilization: the case of British Pakistani Muslims in the UK and Malay Muslims in Singapore

Gabriele Marranci

Abstract

This article discusses, through a comparative approach, the experience of young Muslims in Singapore and the UK as far as integration is concerned. The paper suggests that one of the main issues faced by young Muslims, in both countries, is how they are represented and understood. Indeed, British South Asian Muslims as well as Malay Muslim Singaporeans are still living in a dynamic of postcolonialism. The heritage of British colonialism still, although latently, works through the creation of categories and classifications of how identity should be defined. In both the cases of British South Asian Muslims and Singaporean Malay Muslims, there is often an unspoken request for the imagined ethnic minority to mimic the 'achiever' majority. It is in this dynamic that we can recognize what I have called a 'rhetoric of civilization'.

A critical reflection

The first version of this article contributed to a workshop focusing on the debate surrounding the rights, inclusion and exclusion of Asian ethnic and racial minorities. Although some scholars in Southeast Asia, and particularly in Singapore, may perceive the word 'ethnic' and 'racial' as part of a '*modus vivendi*' of making sense of society,[1] the reality is very complex when observed from a 'human' perspective, as I will try to do in this contribution, rather than solely from a cultural one. Hence, beyond being superfluous, the following paragraphs are necessary to debunk the essentialism which affects much of the discussion of 'minorities' and concepts such as 'native' and 'ethnic', but also 'subjects' and 'citizens' (Wee 2002). My contention in this article is that, despite the multiple differences between the case of British Pakistani Muslims and Singaporean Malay Muslims, their social life is deeply affected by what I have identified as a 'rhetoric of civilization', a consequence of a still not yet exhausted, and deeply rooted, colonial heritage (Bhabha 1994).

Ethnic, minority, subjects and citizens: these words have a clear Greek-Latin origin. Ethnic originated from the ancient Greek *ethnikos* which is linked to the idea of 'nation'; minority from the Latin *minoritas* which implies the state of being a minor; subjects from the Latin *subjectus*, which derives from the past participle *subicere* i.e. *sub*-'under' + *jacere* 'throw', and citizens from the Latin *civitas*, linked to the concept of 'city'. They are words that, as we shall see, have played an essential role in the historical development of what I have called the 'rhetoric of civilization'. These, however, are mainly, geographically and culturally speaking, Western hegemonic terms aimed at a specific political and academic domain. We can agree or disagree with Bourdieu's post-modernism, but we have to recognize, as he did, that labelling is not merely a neutral process of classification that social scientists perform, but rather an act of power, often politically connoted, in relation to the studied minorities and 'others' (Bourdieu 1982). However, beyond the political and academic (and often academically political) power of the label, how many of us in everyday interactions make sense of others and ourselves mainly through such categories? If you meet a colleague, do you immediately think about his or her ethnicity, status as majority/minority or conceptualize his or her position as a 'citizen'? I believe I am safe in arguing that, other than in specific circumstances, the above keywords do not affect our everyday interpersonal interactions; they work, so to say, in the background.

Allow me to observe another aspect: the four terms are polythetic; all of them are utilized for communication and share the power of classifying, marking and creating differences. Thus 'ethnic', 'minority', 'subjects' and 'citizens' are not ontological categories, but rather they exist as ideas which can be shared, passed from person to person or from group to group. In other words, they are mental representations. To illustrate, they are maps attempting to represent a territory; yet, as Alfred Korzybski would have us remember, 'the map is not the territory' (1948, p. 58; Bateson 2000). Nonetheless, in many instances academics have followed the political discourse, forgetting such a simple, but powerful, cognitive distinction. We need to ask, therefore, at which level are we speaking when using the above mentioned keywords: are we discussing the map or conflating the two – and committing a mistake of logical type – by believing that the map *is* the territory, where the idea is equal to the material fact? This fallacy is typical of much political discourse and politicians often end up, by virtue of politics, reinforcing a general perception that what is real and important is the *map*. Unfortunately, during the past fifty years, my own discipline of social anthropology has followed the trend, particularly in the case of the study of ethnic minorities. People, in everyday life and without a specific reason for doing so, do not conceptualize themselves as ethnic, a minority, a subject or even as a citizen of a particular state (and indeed we often have national celebrations in order to remind us about that).

Studying ethnic Muslim minorities through comparative approaches

Studying ethnic minority groups though a comparative approach is not a novelty (see, for instance, Ragin and Hein 1993; Cornwell and Stoddard 2000; Stone and Rutledge 2003), yet there is a clear lack of comparative studies focusing on Western and Southeast Asian realities, in particular as far as Muslims are concerned. I have noticed during my research in Singapore that some scholars have found my comparative approach misdirected, since, they argue, Pakistani and Bangladeshi Muslims in the UK are immigrants while Malay Muslim Singaporeans are natives to the island, or at least certainly far from being immigrants in the region. I strongly disagree with this objection as young Singaporean Malay Muslims and young British South Asian Muslims share not only similar biological developments as humans (Cozolino 2002) but also, living in two globalized and highly cosmopolitan nations, much of the youth culture, such as video games, music, ideas and attitudes (Ferle and Chan 2008). Furthermore, suggesting that the new generations of South Asian Muslims in the UK are migrants, compared to the Malay Muslims in Singapore – and thus ontologically different, according to these scholars – demonstrates a lack of familiarity with the history of South Asian Muslims in the UK, who have been very well rooted in the country since the 1800s (Ansari 2004). Ironically, while modern Singapore, from the time of Sir Thomas Stamford Raffles in 1819, may have contained a small number of Malay villages, it is also true that the vibrantly developing city has attracted many more 'ethnic' Malays from Indonesia and Malaysia as migrants (Shamsul 2001). Finally, it is important, in particular for what I shall discuss below, to notice that both young Malays in Singapore and young South Asians in the UK often have, unfortunately, little knowledge of their own heritage, making their experience of ethnicity, seen as a 'map', very similar.

The relevance of a comparative study of Malay Muslims in Singapore is even clearer if we consider how, as Aljunied has rightly explained, some Singaporean scholars have asserted

> that recent studies of the Malay identity are essentially "irrelevant" because the long-standing boundary markers that define the Malay identity are Islam, the Malay language, and the sense of belonging to the "Malay world." According to this line of reasoning, any scholarly arguments or popular perceptions that do not correspond to the prevailing notions of how a Malay is to be defined must be viewed as part of the colonialist project of representing ethnic groupings in Southeast Asia in ways designed to render their identities ambiguous. (Aljunied 2010, p. 306)

Indeed, there is a strong tension between how 'ethnic minorities' are represented, discussed and imagined and how the single individuals, assumed to be part of such taxonomy, actually perceive themselves in relation to their environment.[2] Rapport has highlighted such a vulnus in social scientific studies and noticed that social sciences tend to regard individual actors 'as put upon' rather than 'putting on.... Questions such as how individuals deal with life, how they make meaning in the midst of everyday life and change, suffering and good fortune, become questions largely of social determination' (2003, p. 52). By contrast, Rapport has suggested the centrality of individuality as far as social action is concerned, since 'it is the individual – in individual energy, creativity, will – that the force of the social and cultural lies' (see 1997, p. 2; 2003, p. 6; Hornborg 2003, p. 98). This viewpoint is extremely relevant to an anthropological study of ethnic minorities in Asia, but also in the West. It is only by paying more attention to the individual and understanding society not as a mysterious, self-achieving, self-controlled mechanism, but rather as consisting of the dynamics of individuals, that we may recognize the cybernetic (i.e. communica-tional) property of what we call society. The main risk of continuing in the study of ethnic minorities with the tendency to 'regard the individual actor as put upon rather than "putting on"' is not only to engage in a flawed social (un)science but also, and more perniciously, potentially to reinforce trends of de-humanization that are so common in our era.

It is for this reason that a comparative approach to the dynamics of exclusion between different minority groups in countries such as the UK and Singapore can help to highlight those common elements affecting today's young people from an ethnic and religious minority background. Yet we cannot discuss ethnic minorities, subjects and citizens without another, very fundamental, keyword: identity.

Identity and the constructivist mistakes

The main paradigm by which identity is understood among social scientists (with few exceptions, see Marranci (2006, 2008)) has been through symbolic interactionism and cultural constructivism, both being forms of culturalism. From this viewpoint, identity and the selves of individuals are the direct consequence of the 'structural logic of that individual's social circumstances. If I am a Nuer, then I must think like a Nuer' (Cohen 1995, p. 1). This perspective may over-emphasize not only social structure, but also the very idea existing in the 1970s, until recent innovative approaches, that non-Western people who share culture would also share consciousness and identity.[3] There is also another weakness in much of the discourse about identity: an often-unclear definition of self, since in many studies and discussions 'identity' and 'self' tend to blur into each other's domain. Further-more, and particularly after the 1980s, starting from the field of cultural studies, identity has been read as 'fleeting, fragmentary, and buffeted', so much that, to use Holland's words, 'from the extreme ephemeralist position, daily life, especially in the post-modern era, is a movement from self to self' (Holland 1997, p. 170).

Reviewing many articles and books dealing with different ethnic minorities, but in particular Muslim ones, I have found myself increasingly thinking of Welsch's words, 'to be healthy today is truly only possible in the form of schizophrenia – if not polyphrenia' (1990, p. 171). Indeed, as Sökefeld has critically observed, 'the question of identity is almost completely detached from the problem of the self. In the vast body of literature about ethnic identity the self is rarely mentioned, and in writings about the self, a relation between the self and identities is sometimes noted but remains unexplored' (1999, p. 419). This is not so surprising when we remember that social structural theories of identity have been widely (though often implicitly) employed as the theoretical framework in these studies and also, as we shall see, in the policy-making surrounding 'ethnic minorities'. In these cases, ethnic minorities are considered to posses identities which are as unstable and fluid as the cultures that allegedly create them.

Yet such a fluid malleability of identity is not the real story, but rather one that helps aim at the possibility of assimilation. In reality, and this is the point of tension, self and identity start from the universal natural elements of being human (Marranci 2006). As I have explained elsewhere, there is a clear distinction between self and identity. In neurobiological terms, evolutionary processes have created different stages of 'self' (Damasio 2000). Human beings posses all the different stages of the self we can find among living beings though with an additional one, the autobiographical self, which is uniquely human. Memory plays a fundamental role in the human self since, in

Damasio's words, 'reactivations and display of selected sets of autobiographical memories' (2000, p. 196) are what form the auto-biographical self, or what normally in everyday life we simply call 'self'. Convincing clinical examples, based on patients with particular types of brain damage, have demonstrated that without autobiographical memories our sense of self (i.e. our sense of past, future and historical-temporal continuity) could not be developed: literally, without it, one loses oneself.

All of this tells us something important about the distinction that exists – and has been so often ignored within the field of social sciences – between self (i.e. autobiographical self in Damasio's terminology) and identity. Indeed, while the self is a real entity in our neurocognitive system, identity is not. According to Damasio, identity 'is a delicately shaped machinery of our imagination [which] stakes the probabilities of selection toward the same, historically continuous self' (1999, p. 225). I fully agree with Damasio's concept of identity.

Yet I suggest that we need to emphasize that identity is a process (Marranci 2006) that allows human beings to make sense of their autobiographical self and, at the same time, to express it, especially through symbols. In this process, emotions (the actual bodily reactions, such as a quickened heartbeat, crying, jumping at a surprise and so on) and feelings (the explanation and way of making sense of the bodily changes, i.e. emotions at a conscious level) are central. I can say that we humans live in a sort of tautological circuit: (1) the environment produces stimuli; (2) which produce emotions (the bodily reactions); (3) which human beings perceive and rationalize as feelings; (4) which affect their autobiographical self; (5) which is experienced through the delicately shaped machinery of their imagination (identities); (6) which is affected by the feelings induced by the emotions. What I have described until now is a circuit of causalities based on information both internal and external to the individual, in other words, an ecological system of identity. This means that a person stating, for instance, 'I am Muslim', in terms of the autobiographical self means 'I feel to be Muslim'. Hence, it is what we feel to be that determines how the 'machinery of our imagination' will '[stake] the probabilities of selection toward the same, historically continuous self' and how it will be presented to others rather than the infinite possibilities of a 'system of symbols'. In other words, Muslims are 'Muslims' as long as they 'feel to be' Muslim, and not because the 'system of symbols' called Islam somehow makes them Muslim.

As we shall see later, this has massive implications for how governments and policy-makers imagine ethnic minorities, how the idea of civilization is understood vis-à-vis ethnic minorities' and citizens' identities, for what is expected from the ethnic minorities to be fully recognized as 'citizens' instead of 'subjects' and for the individual 'feeling of being' which, if I am right in assuming the above, may enter into conflict with the imagined (i.e. the map) reality.

Muslims in the UK: imperfect British?

There are about 1.6 million Muslims in the UK. Although accounting for only 2.7 per cent of the overall population, Islam is the second largest religion of the country after Christianity and the first in growing populations (Census 2001). Furthermore, the concentration of Muslims in major English and Scottish cities, such as London (607,000), Birmingham (192,000), Greater Manchester (125, 219), Bradford-Leeds (150,000) and Glasgow (33,000), make them an important and visible part of UK society; which is more than the statistical 2.7 per cent may represent, particularly if we consider that Pakistani Muslims in Bradford are 14 per cent of the entire city's population. Nonetheless, when we speak of Muslims in the UK it is important to remember that they are not a monolithic entity, but rather highly variegated in ethnicity, nationality and religious affiliations. Although Pakistanis account for 1.2 per cent of the population and make up 43 per cent of Great Britain's Muslims, with Bangladeshis numbering 16 per cent, the remaining 41 per cent of Muslims are neither: they are Indians (8.3 per cent), black Africans (6.1 per cent) and white British (4 per cent) among others. If we break down some of the 'Other' category of the Census 2001, we observe that, according to Peach's analysis (2006, pp. 632–3), white Muslims in England and Wales number around 179,000 (altogether about 12 per cent of the Muslim population), and, beyond the 4 per cent of white British, we find Bosnian, Albanian and Kosovan (about 60,000), Kurdish, Turkish and North African (about 36,000) as well as Middle Easterners (about 93,000). Notwithstanding this diversity, academic studies have focused mainly on Pakistanis and, though less, Bangladeshis.

From the mid-1970s, British politicians and society became aware that what started as a community of work migrants invited to England to facilitate the post-World War II reconstruction would not 'return' to their homeland; they were in the UK to become part of it. This shifted how the host society saw their South Asian populations. With the settlement of the guest workers, Islam became visible and acknowledged as part of their identity. If ethnicity and nationality marked with few exceptions (e.g. Barclay 1969) the first social scientific studies of the mainly South Asian community, today an overwhelming majority of studies have started to feature the word 'Muslim' in their titles and abstracts. This does not mean that the focus on ethnicity and nationality has completely disappeared. At the beginning of the

1980s, many studies were still referring to the ethnic-national identity of these immigrants and their socio-economic status. Nonetheless, the fact that these South Asians had started to define, in the new migration context, their identity as 'Muslim' reinforced the centrality of Islam as their visible element. Islam progressively became also part of the landscape of major British cities through the minarets and the oriental-styled mosques which, for the first time, left the pages of the *One Thousand and One Nights* to materialize in bricks and glass amid the curious, or suspicious, looks of non-Muslim neighbours (Metcalf 1996).

Unsurprisingly, nationality and ethnicity became less relevant to the understanding of Muslim communities. The awareness that the, now redefined, Muslim immigration was a permanent feature of UK society redirected attention to the difficulties that Muslim immigrants had to face in the new environment to maintain their Muslim identity and community and the difficulty that the UK might have in integrating them.

The Census 2001 shows that, in comparison to any other section of British society, Muslims (with little difference among the several ethnic groups and national backgrounds) are on average the most deprived. Not only did they have the highest rate of unemployment, the poorest health and the lowest level of education, but also they were the least likely to own their own homes. Living in such a reality, after more than fifty years of contributing to the UK society, should we be surprised, as some seem to be, that only 65 per cent of Muslims were ready to define their national identity as British, English, Scottish or Welsh? After World War II Muslims coming from South Asian countries became part of the British proletariat. Yet the relationship between white workers, and in particular Pakistani Muslims, was not always an easy one.

Discrimination pushed these new migrants toward an increasing isolation within working-class neighbourhoods, depopulated of their former white population that meanwhile could afford better locations (Lewis 1994). The tendency to see religion as the main element that could prevent Muslims from integrating within the 'modern', 'civilized' and 'secular' Western democracies increased at the end of 1980s. Two events, the less-known Honeyford affair (in 1984) and the evergreen Rushdie affair (in 1989) seemed to confirm a previously alleged incompatibility between what were indicated as 'Western' and 'Islamic' values. For the first time the Western mass media played a central role in shaping the debate on Muslims in the West. Ray Honeyford succeeded in attracting the mass media as well as the angry attention of the English Muslim community. In 1984, Ray Honeyford, who was the headmaster of Drummond Road Middle School, in Bradford, England, published a controversial newspaper article (see

Halstead (1988) and Lewis (1994) for a discussion of the article) asking for the rejection of 'the multi-racial myth'. At the centre of his call for the defence of an alleged 'Britishness' was the rejection of 'barbaric' Islamic customs, symbolized, in this case, by the Islamic slaughtering style. Honeyford referred to it because of the halal meat his school provided to Muslim pupils.

According to him, the 'barbaric' practice, which lacked any British sensitivity, was tolerated in the name of a dangerous politically correct multiculturalism, which would finally kill what he perceived to be more civilized British values. By lamenting the destiny of British cows at the hands of Muslim butchers, he called for an assimilation policy that, through the denial of Muslim children's religious identity, could transform them into perfect 'British subjects'. Despite wide support from the right-wing press and various members of the white middle classes, the South Asian protests and the too-visibly racially motivated argument forced him to take early retirement and to keep his opinions to himself.

The Honeyford affair highlighted the relevance that Islam as a religion and as an expression of identity had not only for the immigrants but also for their children (Halstead 1988; Lewis 1994). In conclusion, if we analyse the Honeyford affair from an anthropological perspective, we can observe that four elements were part of it: religious identity, national identity, community affiliation and, in particular, loyalty. That last term would play a fundamental role in the Rushdie affair. In 1989 *The Satanic Verses* was published and on 14 February 1989 Ayatollah Khomeini responded by issuing a fatwa, albeit an ineffective one, calling for the death of Rushdie, who ended up protected by the British government. If the British government could save Rushdie from the grave, it could not avoid the global Muslim protests that the publication of the book triggered, which culminated in the famous UK book-burning demonstration in Bradford, on 14 January 1989. Journalists and politicians as well as ordinary non-Muslims questioned the 'loyalty' of their Muslim population.

The events of 9/11 have not facilitated the dialogue between the Muslim communities within the UK and the mainstream society. Rather, the perception of Muslims (normally perceived as a monolithic entity) as an enemy within has affected the lives of young Muslims. As Hopkins has observed, 'racism sees the reconstruction of the discourse of "the Asian" reconstituted through the foregrounding of "the Muslim"' (2004, p. 259). Therefore the British Muslim living in the UK has to answer again and again the loyalty question 'Are you British or are you Muslim?', or, in other words, 'Are you one of us?'

The discourse of 'British values' has become increasingly strong in the aftermath of 7/7 together with the idea that Muslims, seen as an overall ethnic minority regardless of ethnicity or nationality, should adopt 'British values' as defined by British politicians and commentators. In addition, Muslims are simultaneously expected to accept a minority status within the 'civilized West', seen no less monolithically as a 'Judaeo-Christian' entity. Melanie Phillips' book *Londonistan* (2006) strongly argues that British values, and the UK itself, are in danger because Muslims 'refuse to *accept minority status* and [insist] instead that their values must trump those of the majority' (2006, p. 28, emphasis added) or because 'playing on the pathological fear of prejudice created by victim culture, Muslims refuse to accept responsibility for Islamist violence, blame the British government instead for siding with America over Afghanistan and Iraq, and denounce any resistance to the imposition of an Islamic perspective as "Islamophobia"' (2006, p. 28). Finally, Phillips concludes with a clear example of the rhetoric of civilization:

> The West is under threat from an enemy that has shrewdly observed the decadence and disarray in Europe, where Western civilisation first began. And the greatest disarray of all is in Britain, the very cradle of Western liberty and democracy, but whose cultural confusion is now plain for all to see in Londonistan.... Whether it will finally pull itself together and stop sleepwalking into cultural oblivion is a question on which the future of the West may now depend. (Phillips 2004, p. 285)

Muslims in the UK are asked to integrate and adopt 'British values', or, in other words, the general rhetoric seems to imply that if, as some even seem to suggest, Muslims are not the 'enemy within', at least they are the 'imperfect British' to be educated and guided towards success, or 'real' civilization. To do so, the British Muslim community must accept 'minority' status or blend, particularly through 'reforming' its identity, within the civilized majority. Identity here, as we have discussed above, is perceived clearly as being culturally constructed, flexible, multiple and easy to modify if the symbols – in this case Islam – are modified too. Here lies the basis of the repetitive calls for a 'reformed' Islam, a 'British Islam'. I am not surprised that such a call for identity 'assimilation' not only remains, with few exceptions, unanswered, but actually provokes resistance. Personal identity, as I have explained, is not symbolically constructed, and 'the British Muslim community' is no more than a political and academic imagination, because Muslims, as we have seen, come from different backgrounds and Islamic approaches.

Muslim Malays in Singapore: imperfect Singaporeans?

In Singapore, Muslim Malays are a minority, accounting in 2009 for about 14 per cent of the overall population (Singapore Department of Statistics 2005, p. viii). However, not so differently from the various ethnic groups forming the Muslim population in the UK, Muslim Malay Singaporeans face challenges in many social indicators when compared to the other two ethnic groups, the Indians (7 per cent of the population) and the majority (77 per cent of the population) Chinese. Among the problems plaguing the 'community' we can cite a monthly household income under the national median, as well as high rates of divorce, teenage pregnancy, unemployment and school dropouts, showing that the Malay families in Singapore are still, despite some visible improvements, struggling to overcome the enduring cycle of underachievement in a society in which achievement is strongly monitored. As Hapipi (2006) has observed, scholars have offered various theories to explain such a grim situation from postcolonial factors (Alatas, S.H. 1972, 1977; Li 1989; Alatas, S.F. 2003; Rahman and Aishah 2006; Aljunied 2010) to ethnic differentiation and cultural/ biological deficit policies (Li 1989; Rahim 1999; Lai 1995; Suratman 2004) and from coping strategies in facing diversity (Zoohri 1987; Stimpfl 1997) to post Malaysian-separation experience and adjust-ment (Li 1989; Tarmugi 1992) among many others.

Another similarity with the British reality is how Malays in Singapore (but also the Chinese and the Indians) have been seen as a monolithic ethnic and religious category (Chua 2007) despite the fact that, underneath the politically defined umbrella of 'Malay', there are different ethnic groups such as the Javanese, Minangkabau, Baewa-nese, Acehnese and the Malay. In the case of Singapore, however, this has been institutionalized through the so-called CMIO (Chinese, Malay, Indian and Others) social-political (they are marked on ID cards) identities.[4] Such a bureaucratization of 'race' is a legacy of the British colonial period; however, it has been re-engineered to serve the 'hard multiculturalism' model under which Singapore has flourished since its dramatic split with Malaysia in 1965 (Vasu 2008). In this model of multiculturalism, management of communities is essential to avoiding dangerous friction that may threaten the religious and ethnic harmony within the city state. This essentialization of each community is clearly celebrated during, for instance, Racial Harmony Day (on the 21st of July), on which students in Singaporean schools are encour-aged to dress, present food and dance according to the community identifier recorded on their ID card. It is clear that the historical memory, which the government reinforces and maintains, of the racial tension which shook Singapore from the 1950s to the 1960s (the so-called Maria Hertogh Riots in 1950 and the Prophet Muhammad Birthday Riots in 1964 for example) has, differently from in the UK, linked the survival of the city state to the level of 'tolerance' achieved among its ethnic components.[5]

Therefore, Chua (2003) has convincingly demonstrated that Singapore's vision of multiculturalism aims to be a powerful instrument of social control. Indeed, although Article 152(2) of the Singapore Constitution recognized the Singaporean Malays as the indigenous people of the island, both the multicultural policies and the PAP[6] government's emphasis on meritocracy have prevented the Malays from being able to derive any privilege, as an ethnic group, from their status as indigenous people, since it is the main goal of the government that all the ethnic groups are treated equally, with the only differences deriving from personal meritocratic and, in particular, communitarian achievements.

However, as other studies have highlighted (see Chua 2003; Vasu 2008; especially Barr and Low 2005), there is a variable that is often played down in the discourse of ethnic Singapore: the majority of the ethnic Chinese. Ironically, the same hard multiculturalism which guarantees that Malays (and Indians) are nearly proportionally represented in the Singaporean parliament through the so-called Greater Representative Constituency (GRC)[7] also guarantees the political predominance of the Chinese. So too demographically, since, as Chua has noted, 'Given geopolitical conditions, the government has made a fetish out of changing demographics and has decided that the Chinese population should constitute approximately three-quarters of the total population at all times' (2003, p. 69).

As Vasu has emphasized, although CMIO is aimed at racial harmony, it also facilitates the perpetuation of racial stereotypes since 'creating a category requires that it be filled with content' (2008, p. 29). This is particularly visible in the case of stereotypes affecting the Malay community, many of which have colonial origins and some of which are even rooted in unproved, imagined biological bias (Kopnina 2004), so that Malays may be represented – and not just in popular parlance – as 'endowed with traits of complacency, indolence, apathy, infused with a love of leisure and an absence of motivation and discipline' (Rahim 1998, p. 49). This colonial, but still present, representation has facilitated the simplistic idea that Malay Muslims are predisposed towards drug addiction, criminality, teenage pregnancy and family dysfunction and are consequently unable to perform as well as other racial groups in the Singaporean competitive social market.

By contrast, positive stereotyping presents Chinese Singaporeans as the 'quintessential "economic beings", natural entrepreneurs predisposed to seek pro?t at every opportunity' (Kopnina 2004, p. 249). In this stereotypical imagination – which is totally oblivious to the fragmented reality of Chinese Singaporeans, the struggles of some as well as inter-Chinese discrimination[8] – the astonishing Singaporean economic and social success is to be attributed to the 'Chinese way', from which the other ethnic groups, particularly the Malay, have to learn and with which, most importantly, they must assimilate (Barr and Low 2005). Some attempts to transform the perception into political philosophy in the country failed during the 1980s, such as the proposal to use Confucianism as a state ideology – an idea which, however, saw a revamp when a discussion on 'Asian values' finally informed the 1991 *White Paper on Shared Values* (see Chua 1998, pp. 196–7).

Of course, this is an unspoken, and I would say subliminal, message, which surfaces in political discourse only by accident or through very rare 'paternalistic' advice).[9] Yet, in the case of the general Chinese population, this perception and representation are increasingly less unspoken and more visible. Furthermore, the event of 9/11 and, in December 2001 and August 2002, the arrest of thirty-four members of the terrorist organization *Jemaah Islamiyah* in Singapore, among whom there were Muslim Singaporeans, for planning bomb attacks throughout Singapore, intensified and renewed the old issue of Singaporean Malay Muslim loyalty (one of the reasons for which, until recently, Singaporean Malay Muslims could not join the armed forces). Fear started to shape perceptions of the Muslim 'Other' within the city state, and the press started to record minor, but significant, incidents such as 'a sarong-wearing man being visibly shunned; a Singapore Chinese resolution not to get into the same lift as a Malay; the proud claim of a taxi driver that she will not pick up a Malay fare; to parents who insisted their children be transferred out of a class with a tudung-wearing teacher' (Ismail and Shaw 2006, p. 41).

During my research with young Malay Muslims I have noticed two distinct ways in which they perceive their community. On the one hand, the majority of my respondents have absorbed the overwhelming rhetoric of a Malay community plagued by trouble and lagging behind the 'Singaporean standard'. On the other, however, there is a shared awareness that Singapore is a 'Chinese' country and not a Malay one. As one of my respondents stated, 'we are the indigenous population of Singapore. The English acknowledged this and the Singaporean Constitution acknowledges this. But, we are not Singaporean enough. To be a real Singaporean, we must be Chinese in our way of thinking and working. If you are not, you are just an indigenous.' I am also not surprised that Malay MPs seem to have the lowest level of support and are often described as *Pak Turut* (i.e. servile). A very worrying aspect is that a significant number young Malay Singaporeans do not seem overly concerned about the perceived assimilation within a 'Chinese way of life' since many are 'detached' from the very idea of Singapore and prefer instead to emphasize their 'global' identity, which is often marked by a 'Western' lifestyle that is antagonistic to the 'Chinese' one. Many young Malay Muslims have expressed the intention to leave Singapore, if given the opportunity, in order to move to Australia, the US or Europe (particularly the UK).

As in the case of the South Asian Muslims in the UK, Malay Muslims in Singapore face a tension between an ethnic, religious and, in general, stereotyped identity that is socially imposed upon them as well as the actual personal identity, the 'feeling to be'. Some of the younger generation of Malays, faced with a prospect of continuing to perceive themselves as 'subjects' inside a managed multiculturalism and moving further towards the silent, but persistent, assimilation within a Singaporean-ness which inevitably will have its ethos within an imagined 'Chinese way' of life, may choose the 'global' dimension, in which, more often than not, criminal activities, drugs and teen pregnancies together with family instability are just part of the ordinary, although undesired, landscape.

The rhetoric of civilization

At the beginning of this article the implications of our four keywords – ethnic, minority, subjects and citizens – were discussed. We have seen that, although they are not 'real' material things, they of course have the power to interact with, but not fully to determine, people's lives. In both the cases of Muslims in the UK, particularly when South Asian, and Malay Muslims in Singapore, we have observed a 'discourse of values' which assumes an 'ethos' through which the idea of civic society is, or is supposed to be, expressed. We have to recognize that in both countries (but inevitably in a majority of countries, regardless of their political machinery) the 'ethos' is shaped by the idea of an 'ethnic' majority. Personal identities are forgotten in this process or even denied to the advantage of a simplified, and often stereotyped, communitarianism. It is in this fertile ground that a 'rhetoric of civilization' takes shape. This rhetoric has a prize at stake: the power of defining how to be human, and consequently who is human. Part of the 'rhetoric of civilization' process is the questioning of the other, particularly about loyalty – 'Are you one of us?'

In reality this is a rhetorical question of denial, a rhetorical question of ostracism-it dichotomizes 'otherness' by transforming difference into 'culpability'. This is a process that could easily transubstantiate into persecution, with the Holocaust being a well-known example. Today, in the majority of cases, rather than being worn on clothes, 'yellow stars' take the form of re-imagined, stereotyped, imposed, social identities which deny, or ignore, individual freedom. This imposition forces the person into a cage of objectification in which restraints have been imposed on the expression of their identity affirmation, the 'feeling to be'. This process has contributed to a new, postmodern, neo-colonial freak show where the 'abnormal' and the 'deviant' can be identified and falsely abstracted as a specific 'community'. Indeed, it is only though the denial of the individual, the *persona*, that the stereotype can be formed and used. However, this can only be a culturalist illusion as success is not collective. Success, no less than integration and action, can only be individually based; individuals make a difference for better or worse.

Bhabha (1994) has suggested that stereotyping is not only a fixed representation of the subject in the construction of the colonial 'other', but also a process similar to fetishism. 'The fetish or stereotype gives access to an "identity" which is predicated as much on mastery and pleasure as it is on anxiety and defence, for it is a form of multiple and contradictory beliefs in its recognition of difference and the disavowal of it' (1994, p. 75). In this complex process, contradictions between the known and imagined become the reality of representation. In other words, the object is understood not in its integrity but as metonymy. Bhabha has emphasized how the identity of the 'other' becomes fetishized not for the sake of false representation which may become 'the scapegoat of discrimination', but for 'the fantasy that dramatizes the impossible desire for a pure, undifferentiated origin' of the colonizer (1994, p. 81).

British South Asian Muslims as well as Malay Muslim Singaporeans are still living in a dynamic of postcolonialism. Indeed, the heritage of British colonialism still, although latently, works through the creation of categories and classifications of how identity should be defined. In both the cases of British South Asian Muslims and Malay Muslims in Singapore, there is the often unspoken request for the imagined ethnic minority to mimic the 'achiever'. Again Bhabha has observed that this 'mimicry is the desire for a reformed, recognizable Other, *as subject of a difference that is almost the same,* but not quite, which is to say, that the discourse of mimicry is constructed around an ambivalence; in order to be effective mimicry it must continually produce its slippage, its excess, its difference' (1994, p. 86, emphasis in original). The ultimate risk of this process is that some members of the ethnic minority may feel to be almost British, almost Singaporean – but not quite.

Notes

1.   Note that in Singapore ethnicity has been institutionalized through a rather rigid CMIO (Chinese, Malay, Indian and Others) ethnic identity classification which marks the official political position on social identities (see Chua 2007).
2.   By environment I mean here both the actual physical space as well as the interaction taking place within it and also the objects, material and conceptual, which one may meet within it.
3.   Just to mention some examples: Chodorow (1978); Dumont (1970); Geertz (1975) Lykes (1985); Marsella, De Vos and Hsu (1985); Sampson (1985); Shweder and LeVine (1984); Triandis (1989).
4.   It is important to note here that, in the case of the category 'Indian', this even includes Pakistanis and Bangladeshis.
5.   For a critique of the political exploitation of these riots by the Singaporean government, see Aljunied (2009, 2010).
6.   People's Action Party, which has ruled Singapore since 1959.
7.   For more about the GRC and the mechanism behind it see Chua (2003) and Vasu (2008).
8.   For more, see Hefner (1998) as well as Benton and Gomez (2001).
9.   Lee Kuan Yew, for instance, described a Malay successful in business as 'acting just like a Chinese. You know, he's bouncing, running around, to-ing and fro-ing' (quoted in Han, Fernandez and Tan 1998, p. 184).

References

ALATAS, SYED HUSSAIN 1972 *Modernisation and Social Change*, Sydney: Angus & Robertson
────── 1977 *The Myth of the Lazy Natives*, London: Frank Cass
ALATAS, SYED FARID 2003 'Sociology of the Malays', in C.K. Tong and K.F. Lian (eds), *The Making of Singapore Sociology: Society and State*, Singapore: Times Academic Press
ALJUNIED, SYED MUHD KHAIRUDIN 2009 *Colonialism, Violence and Muslims in Southeast Asia: The Maria Hertogh Controversy and its Aftermath*, London: Routledge
────── 2010 'Ethnic resurgence, minority communities, and state policies in a network society: the dynamics of Malay identity formation in postcolonial Singapore', *Identities*, vol. 17, nos 2–3, pp. 304–26
ANSARI, HUMAYUN 2004 *'The Infidel Within':Muslims in Britain Since 1800*, London: Hurst
BARCLAY, HAROLD 1969 'The perpetuation of Muslim tradition in the Canadian north', *Muslim World*, vol. 59, pp. 64–73
BARR, MICHAEL and LOW, JENVON 2005 'Assimilation as multiracialism: the case of Singapore's Malays', *Asian Ethnicity*, vol. 6, no. 3, pp. 161–82
BATESON, GREGORY 2000 *Steps to an Ecology of Mind*, Chicago, IL: Chicago University Press
BENTON, GREGOR and GOMEZ, EDMUND 2001 *Chinatown and Transnationalism: Ethnic Chinese in Europe and Southeast Asia*, Occasional Paper, Centre for the Study of the Chinese Southern Diaspora, Australian National University, Canberra
BHABHA, HOMI 1994 *The Location of Culture*, London and New York: Routledge

BOURDIEU, PIERRE 1982 *Ce Que Parler Veut Dire*, Paris: Fayard

CHODOROW, NANCY 1978 *The Reproduction of Mothering: Psychoanalysis and the Sociology of Gender*, Berkeley: University of California Press

CHUA, BENG HUAT 1998 'Culture, multiracialism, and national identity in Singapore', in Kuan-Hsing Chen (ed.), *Trajectories: Inter-Asia Cultural Studies*, London and New York: Routledge

—— 2003 'Multiculturalism in Singapore: an instrument of social control', *Race & Class*, vol. 44, no. 3, pp. 58–77

—— 2007 "Multiracialism as official policy: a critique of the management of difference in Singapore", in Norman Vasu (ed.), *Social Resilience in Singapore: Reflections from the London Bombings*, Singapore: Select Books

COHEN, ANTHONY PAUL 1995 'Introduction', in Cohen Anthony and Rapport Nigel (eds), *Questions of Consciousness*, New York and London: Routledge, pp. 1–20

CORNWELL, GRANT and STODDARD, EVE (eds) 2000 *Global Multiculturalism: Comparative Perspectives on Ethnicity, Race, and Nation*, Lanham, MD: Rowman & Littlefield

COZOLINO, LOUIS 2002 *The Neuroscience of Psychotherapy: Building and Rebuilding the Human Brain*, New York: Norton

DAMASIO, ANTONIO 2000 *The Feeling of what Happens: Body, Emotion and the Making of Consciousness*, London: Vintage

DUMONT, LOUIS 1970 *Homo Hierarchicus*, Chicago, IL: University of Chicago Press

FERLE, LA CARRIE and CHAN, KARA 2008 'Determinants for materialism among adolescents in Singapore', *Young Consumers*, vol. 9, no. 3, pp. 201–14

GEERTZ, CLIFFORD 1975 'On the nature of anthropological understanding', *American Scientist*, vol. 63, pp. 47–53

GERGEN, KENNETH 1968 'Personal consistency and the presentation of self', in Chad Gordon and Kenneth Gergen (eds), *The Self in Social Interaction: Classic and Contemporary Perspectives*, New York: Wiley, pp. 17–56

HALSTEAD, M. 1988 *Education, justice, and cultural diversity: An examination of the Honeyford affair, 1984–85*, London: Falmer Press

HAN, FOOK KWANG, FERNANDEZ, WARREN and TAN, SUMIKO 1998 *Lee Kuan Yew: The Man and His Ideas*, Singapore: Singapore Press Holdings, Times Editions

HAPIPI, RAFIZ MOHYI 2006 "Introduction", in Rafiz Mohyi Hapipi Yayasan, *MENDAKI Policy Digest 2006*, Singapore: MENDAKI, pp. 1–11

HEFNER, R.OBERT 1998 'Introduction', in Robert Hefner (ed.), *Market Cultures: Society and Morality in the New Asian Capitalisms*, Boulder, CO: Westview Press

HOLLAND, DOROTHY 1997 'Selves as cultured, as told by an anthropologist who lacks a soul', in Ashmore Richard and Jussim Lee (eds), *Self and Identity*, New York and Oxford: Oxford University Press, pp. 160–90

HOPKINS, P. 2004 'Young muslim men in Scotland: inclusions and exclusions', *Children's Geographies*, vol. 2, no. 2, pp. 257–72

HORNBORG, ALF 2003 'From animal masters to ecosystem services: exchange, person-hood, and human ecology', in Andreas Roepstorff, Nils Bubandt and Kalevi Kull (eds), *Imagining Nature: Practices of Cosmology and Identity*, Oakville, CT: Aarhus University Press

ISMAIL, RAHIL and SHAW, BRIAN 2006 'Singapore's Malay-Muslim minority: social identification in a post-9/11 world', *Asian Ethnicity*, vol. 7, no. 1, pp. 37–51

KOPNINA, HELEN 2004 'Cultural hybrids or ethnic fundamentalists? Discourses on ethnicity in Singaporean SMEs', *Asian Ethnicity*, vol. 5, no. 2, pp. 245–57

KORZYBSKI, A. 1948 *Science and sanity: An introduction to non-Aristotelian systems and general semantics*, International non-Aristotelian library. Lakeville, Conn: International Non-Aristotelian Library Pub. Co.

LAI, AHENG 1995 *Meanings of Multiethnicity: A Case Study of Ethnicity and Ethnic Relations in Singapore*, Kuala Lumpur: Oxford University Press

LEWIS, PHILIP 1994 *Islamic Britain: Religion, Politics and Identity among British Muslims*, London: I. B. Taurus

LI, TANIA 1989 *Malays in Singapore: Culture, Economy, and Ideology*, Singapore: Oxford University Press

LYKES, BRINTON 1985 'Gender and individualistic vs. collectivist bases for notions about the self', in Abigail Stewart and Brinton Lykes (eds), *Gender and Personality: Current Research on Theory and Research,* Durham, NC: Duke University Press, pp. 268–98

MARRANCI, GABRIELE 2006 *Jihad beyond Islam*, Oxford: Berg

—— 2008 *The Anthropology of Islam*, London and New York: Berg

MARSELLA, ANTHONY, DE VOS, GEORGE and HSU, FRANCIS 1985 *Culture and Self*, London: Tavistock

METCALF, BARBARA (ed.) 1996 *Making Muslim Space in Northern America and Europe*, Berkeley: California University Press

PEACH, CERI 2006 'Muslims in the 2001 Census of England and Wales: gender and economic disadvantage', *Ethnic and Racial Studies*, vol. 29, no. 4, pp. 629–55

PHILLIPS, MELANIE 2006 *Londonistan: How Britain is Creating a Terror State from Within*, London: Gibson Square

RAGIN, CHARLES and HEIN, JEREMY (eds) 1993 'The comparative study of ethnicity: methodological and conceptual issues', in John Stanfield and Dennis Rutledge (eds), *Race and Ethnicity in Research Methods*, Newbury Park, CA: Sage, pp. 254–72

RAHIM, LILY ZUBAIDA 1999 *The Singapore Dilemma: The Political and Educational Marginality of the Malay Community*, Kuala Lumpur: Oxford University Press

RAHMAN, NOOR and AISHAH, ABDUL 2006 *Colonial Image of Malay Adat Laws*, Boston, MA: Brill

RAPPORT, NIGEL 1997 *Transcendent Individual: Towards a Literary and Liberal Anthropology*, London: Routledge

—— 2003 *I Am Dynamite: An Alternative Anthropology of Power*, London and New York: Routledge

SAMPSON, EDWARD 1985 'The decentralisation of identity: toward a revised concept of personal and social order', *American Psychologist*, vol. 40, pp. 1203–11

SHAMSUL, AMRI 2001 'A history of an identity, an identity of a history: the idea and practice of "Malayness" in Malaysia Reconsidered', *Journal of Southeast Asian Studies*, vol. 32, no. 3, pp. 355–66

SHWEDER, RICHARD and LE VINE, ROBERT (eds) 1984 *Culture Theory: Essays on Mind, Self, and Emotion*, Cambridge: Cambridge University Press, pp. 137–57

SINGAPORE DEPARTMENT OF STATISTICS 2005 *The General Household Survey*

SOKEFELD, MARTIN 1999 'Debating self, identity, cultural anthropology', *Current Anthropology*, vol. 40, no. 4, pp. 417–47

STIMPFL, JOSEPH 1997 'Growing up Malay in Singapore', *Southeast Asian Journal of Social Science*, vol. 25, no. 2, pp. 117–38

STONE, JOHN and RUTLEDGE, DENNIS (eds) 2003 *Race and Ethnicity: Comparative and Theoretical Approaches*, Malden, MA: Blackwell

SURATMAN, S.URIANI 2004 *'Problematic Singapore Malays': The Making of a Portrayal*, Singapore: NUS Department of Malay Studies

TARMUGI, ABDULLAH 1992 *Development of the Malay Community in Singapore: Prospects and Problems*, Singapore: NUS Department of Malay Studies

TRIANDIS, H. 1989 'The self and social behavior in differing cultural contexts', *Psychological Review*, vol. 96, no. 3, pp. 506–20

VASU, NORMAN 2008 '(En)countering terrorism: multiculturalism and Singapore', *Asian Ethnicity*, vol. 9, no. 1, pp. 17–32

WEE, WAN LING 2002 'From universal to local culture: the state, ethnic identity, and capitalism in Singapore', in Wee Wan Ling (ed.), *Local Cultures and the 'New Asia'*, Singapore: Institute of Southeast Asian Studies, pp. 129–57

WELSCH, W. 1990 *Ästhetisches Denken*, Stuttgart: P. Reclam

ZOOHRI, WAN HUSSEIN 1987 'Socio-economic problems of the Malays in Singapore', *Sojourn*, vol. 2, no. 2, pp. 178–208

Informal citizens: graduated citizenship in Southern Thailand

Duncan McCargo

Abstract

Drawing on extensive fieldwork conducted in the Southern border region of Thailand, this article explores ways in which Malay Muslims understand their place in Thai society. It argues that a new conception of 'informal citizenship' is needed in order to characterize such relationships between ethnic minorities and the state. The informal Thai citizenship neither sought by, nor granted to, Malay Muslims has parallels with earlier forms of 'graduated citizenship' that applied to the Sino-Thai community for much of the twentieth century. Citizenship is not an either/or, but a matter of degree.

Citizenship is often seen as a simple question of nationality: people either are, or are not, citizens of a given country. This article seeks to question that assumption, arguing instead that informal notions of citizenship may loom just as large as formal notions. In Thailand, the Chinese minority experienced forms of 'graduated citizenship' for much of the twentieth century, enjoying Thai nationality but deprived of voting and other rights. Today, Malay Muslims in Thailand's Southern border provinces are Thai nationals, but do not meet the informally-understood criteria for full Thai citizenship.

Malay Muslims and the South

Around 1.3 million Malay Muslims reside in the Southern 'border' provinces of Pattani, Yala, and Narathiwat, which have a total population of around 1.8 million. Malay Muslims form a majority within their own quite sizeable region, which Chaiwat Satha-Anand has described (echoing Benedict Anderson) as an 'imagined land' (Satha-Anand 2009). Yet, despite their majority status locally, Malay Muslims are permanently labelled as a minority within Thailand's 65 million population, which is more than 90 per cent Buddhist. In fact, 'Malay Muslim' is far from being a homogenous category, but a catch-all and constructed identity (Barnard 2004; Montesano and Jory 2007). These Southern provinces have been the site of a major insurgency since 2004, in which more than 4,200 people have been killed; the imagined land is closely associated for many with serious political violence (for background see International Crisis Group 2005, Askew 2008, and McCargo 2008).

Malay Muslims form a minority group within Thailand's wider Muslim minority, numerically significant but structurally marginalized. Malay Muslims are alienated from so-called 'Thai Muslims' in other parts of the country. Thai Muslims are an influential group in Bangkok, closely tied to political and other elites. The Bunnag family, Shia Muslims of Persian descent, played central roles in Siam's administration and the economy for much of the nineteenth century. General Sonthi Boonyaratglin, a Thai Muslim, commanded the Royal Thai Army (2005–2007) and led the 19 September 2006 military coup against the government of Thaksin Shinawatra. The Chularajamontri – the royally appointed 'spiritual leader' of Thailand's Muslims – always came from central Thailand, and before 1945, office-holders were all Shia rather than Sunni (Yusuf 2010, pp. 37–40).[1] Through institutions such as the Chularajamontri and a structure of provincial Islamic councils, the Thai monarchy and state have sought to secure the loyalty of the Muslim minority and to manage its participation in wider Thai society (McCargo 2010, pp. 94–7). Yet, while such mechanisms have been relatively successful in respect of Thai Muslims, they have largely failed in respect of Malay Muslims.

Malay Muslims see Thai Muslims as over-assimilated, less devout, and too willing to embrace or tolerate negative features of Thai society. One informant told me that if his daughter married a Muslim from Bangkok, it would be almost as bad as her marrying a Buddhist.[2] The Southern border provinces constitute what another informant referred to as a 'dinosaur island',[3] a region characterized by a powerful concoction of pride and parochialism. Viewed as *khaek* (a broadly pejorative term for South Asian or Malay foreigners) by Bangkok Thais, they were typically regarded as 'Thai buffaloes' by Malaysian Malays. In other words, rejected as marginal by both fellow Thai and by fellow Malays, Malay Muslims of Thai nationality have fallen back on their self-generated identity resources, choosing to assert their specific regional characteristics rather than subordinate themselves to broader notions of nationality.

At the heart of the Southern violence lie contrasting views of identity and citizenship. Many Western views of citizenship are heavily indebted to T. H. Marshall's arguments, which classify citizenship into three core components: civil; political; and social (Marshall 1950). Marshall's is a richly historically-informed analysis, viewing citizenship as emerging in phases through a series of compromises and developments. However, Bryan Turner has argued that Marshall's view of citizenship reflects his experience in a relatively homogenous society, and does not capture the complexity of a modern state characterized by ethnic divisions. Nor does Marshall distinguish between active and passive citizenship (Turner 2001, p. 191). Turner argues that recent socio-economic and political changes, including globalization, have led to an 'erosion' of earlier notions of citizenship in societies such as Britain (2001, p. 203). He calls for a re-expanded notion of citizenship that includes a broader range of rights. However, many countries have yet to construct the kinds of citizenship that are now declining in the developed world. It will be argued here that a legal-rational definition of citizenship, even the kind of updated and highly-nuanced version articulated by Turner, is inadequate to explain the realities of countries such as Thailand. In these countries, Marshall's three elements – which might collectively be termed 'formal' citizenship – fail adequately to capture the relationship between the individual and the state. While some scholars have sought to isolate 'cultural citizenship' as an additional component of citizenship based on ideas of multiculturalism, this model originates in a Western context, and is primarily designed to address issues such as immigration and rights of indigenous groups (Miller 2002). In non-Western societies, equal attention must be paid to informal citizenship, notions of identity that supplement legal-rational criteria for being considered a full citizen. While much of the more radically-inspired debate about citizenship addresses questions concerning the 'right to have rights', linked to notions of 'inclusive citizenship' (Kabeer 2005), such perspectives are often essentially normative. Other authors argue that ethnic and social diversity should be reflected in 'differentiated citizenship' (Young 1989, p. 258), an argument normally linked to calls for special treatment and recognition of marginalized groups and communities. Critics of these calls suggest that differentiated citizenship will undermine national and social cohesion, and have detrimental long-term consequences (Kymlicka and Norman 1995, pp. 306–7).

The case of Malay Muslims in Southern Thailand offers a means of elucidating issues often occluded in most of the literature on citizenship. While the literature often assumes, rather idealistically, that minority groups would like to exercise full citizenship rights, many Malay Muslims in Thailand are rather reluctant to participate in a broader society from which they feel deeply alienated. Thai Buddhists (generally known in the deep South as *Thai phut*) are distinguished verbally and often in terms of language choice from Malay Muslims (*nayu*, in local Pattani Malay, *khon melayu* in Thai). These linguistic devices illustrate the identity cleavage between the two communities. Thai Buddhists persistently claim that elements of the Malay Muslim community are disloyal to the Thai state, failing to appreciate the benefits of what Buddhists generally construct and perceive as benevolent and positive rule from Bangkok. Buddhists are generally critical of these 'separatist' tendencies, and view religious and social practices (such as veiling) as evidence of a policy of differentiation and separation practised by Malay Muslims. Reciprocally, for Malay Muslims the discourse of 'us' and 'them' is one derived from Thai Buddhist attitudes and behaviours. Malay Muslims are invited and expected to partake in a wider Thai society which they find unwelcoming, suspicious, patronizing, and deeply unsympathetic. Under such circumstances, it is unsurprising that Malay Muslims are often preoccupied with delineating their own religious and cultural space, seeking to curtail what they see as the intrusions of the Bangkok Buddhist nation-state into their own sphere. For them, neighbouring Malaysia offers an important non-Western example of differentiated, consociational citizenship, in which ethnic Malays and *bumiputera* ('sons of the soil', or indigenous peoples) have been granted explicit economic and employment privileges under the New Economic Policy. These policies reflect what former Malaysian Prime Minister Mahathir Mohamad termed 'The Malay Dilemma': without some redistributive privileges, ethnic Malays would remain economically marginalized, yet a systematic process of positive discrimination could have negative consequences in the longer term, creating a privileged and enfeebled group (Mohamad 1970, pp. 113–14). By contrast, Thai Buddhists profess to advocate undifferentiated citizenship, in which there are no explicit ethnic privileges, but in practice, Thailand is characterized by sharply-differentiated modes of (albeit, informal) citizenship that privilege certain groups.

Given the predominant discourse of 'Thai-ness' and the determination of the country's nation-building elite to suppress all notions of ethnic difference, ethnic minorities fit uncomfortably within modern Thailand (Connors 2007, pp. 128–52). Since 'ethnic Thais' (whatever that means) can only constitute a minority in a nation where those of Lao, Chinese, Malay, Lanna (Northern Thai/Lao), Mon, Vietnamese, Khmer, and other groups are so numerous, the construction of Thai identity is a quietly repressive process, forcing much of Thailand's population to conceal, deny, or play down their underlying cultural and ethnic origins. All of these groups have actively or at least passively subsumed their culture and identity to Thai-ness, which serves as a totalizing discourse. Not for Thailand were Indonesian notions of 'unity in diversity'; for most of the twentieth century, the

Thai equivalent would have been 'unity in similarity', despite the highly-constructed nature of that similarity. However, cultural diversity has been widely recognized as official policy in the 2000s.

The contrast with Chinese-ness

Until recently, there was widespread popular insistence that ethnic differences do not exist in Thailand. In 2000, I organized a seminar in Leeds at which a visiting Thai academic presented a paper on the ethnic Chinese in Northeast Thailand (Nareerat 2000). The seminar was attended by a number of Thai students from the engineering and science faculties, several of whom protested that there were no 'Chinese' people in Thailand: 'everyone in Thailand is Thai'. The students making these claims – mainly university lecturers studying at the doctoral level on government scholarships – all had strikingly Sino-Thai features. The event was an example of the homogenizing, totalizing form of state and popular discourse about Thai-ness. Viewed negatively, the episode illustrated the extent to which young Sino-Thais were in denial about their 'real' ethnicity; at the same time, it revealed the remarkable successes achieved by the promoters of 'Thai-ness'.

While Thailand is often held up as a positive example of Chinese assimilation into a Southeast Asian society, the reality is rather more nuanced and complicated. In fact, Thailand long had a system of 'graduated citizenship' for those of Chinese descent, captured by the differences between terms such as *'chuea chat'*, *'sanchat'*, and *'tang dao'*.[4] Thai laws on naturalization and nationality were rather liberal; during the early decades of the twentieth century, locally-born Chinese gained automatic Thai nationality and after five years of residence, a Chinese migrant of 'good character' and financially secure could apply for naturalization (Skinner 1957, p. 250). But this was not the whole story: after the end of absolute monarchy in 1932, only those Chinese meeting stringent educational or employment requirements were entitled to vote or to stand for electoral office (Coughlin 1960, pp. 177–81). During the Phibun era non-Thais, which meant primarily the Chinese, were excluded from various trades and professions. Between 1953 and 1956 short-lived, legal changes meant that children born to two Chinese parents were now non-Thai, while those born to an alien father were no longer eligible for military service. Thus the rights to vote, to run for electoral office, to enter military service, and to pursue particular professions were all contingent and graduated rights, which were not identical with the holding of Thai nationality; even Thai nationality itself was subject to revocation. However, as Skinner (1957) tellingly observes: 'It is an interesting feature of Thai psychology that no matter how strong the prejudice against "those Chinese", the Thai are never inclined to reject anyone of Chinese ancestry who speaks and behaves like a Thai' (p. 381). In other words, Thai citizenship might be viewed on two parallel and graduated dimensions: a legal dimension based on formal status and rights, and an informal dimension based on attitude, self-presentation, and behaviour

Kasian Tejapira has argued that the ethnic Chinese in Thailand suffer from what he terms 'Thai deficiency syndrome': they feel their own identity to be inferior to Thai identity, and are constantly aspiring to increase their own sense of Thai-ness (Tejapira 2009, p. 271). At the same time, since the 1980s there has been a resurgence of pride in being of Chinese descent. Many have intermarried with Thais and become *lukjin*, literally 'descendants of the Chinese', a 'culturally intermediate Sino-Thai community' (Kasian 1992, p. 117). Prominent historian Suchit Wongthes memorably described this identity as '*jek bon lao*', Lao-ness overlaid with Chinese-ness.

Michelle Tan has suggested that the wealthy Sino-Thais seek to 'boost' their Thai-ness through engaging in donations to royal charities, and to leading Buddhist temples (rather than 'Chinese' temples), and through marriage with elite Thais, especially Thais descended from royal lineage or noble families (Tan forthcoming). In other words, Chinese-ness remains an unsatisfactory basis for identity, one in need of modification and refinement. However, through hybridization, re-branding, and strategic alliances, being *lukjin* has also become a form of cultural asset, one which is essentially compatible with Thai-ness, although it remains a structurally-subordinate form of identity. Kasian Tejapira has discussed how the People's Alliance for Democracy, a pro-monarchist movement which played a pivotal political role between 2006 and 2009, mobilized Sino-Thai support using the slogan '*lukjin rak chat*' [Sino-Thais love the nation] (Kasian 2009, p. 264). Implicitly, Sino-Thais were urged to demonstrate their Thai-ness by defending the monarchy against forces associated with former Prime Minister Thaksin Shinawatra, many of whose supporters were Laos and Khmers from the Northeast of the country. These recent developments support an important argument by Callahan, who previously suggested that 'neo-nationalism now not only includes Sino-Thai but is largely formulated by them' (2003, p. 510).

As Saskia Sassen has argued more broadly, individuals 'can move between multiple meanings of citizenship' (Sassen 2006, p. 188). Some aspects of citizenship 'do not fit the categories and indicators used to capture participation in political life' (2006, p. 193). This article responds to Sassen's call to bridge the considerable distance between theories of citizenship and empirical realities. In the end, Thai-ness is a be-all-and-end-all, an identity that trumps mere Thai nationality. Nationality and citizenship are legal notions, but to understand how sense of belonging and affinity actually work, legal concepts are quite inadequate. Most minority groups in Thailand do enjoy legal citizenship rights, but 'Thai-ness' remains a less accessible status. Other ethnic groups in Thailand experience Thai deficiency syndrome to varying degrees. Northeasterners, for example, often seek to tone down their Lao-ness, adopting the hybridized, recently-constructed identity of *khon isan*, which does not challenge the overarching superiority of Thai-ness. The Northeast was a site of resistance to Bangkok during the immediate post-war period, but this resistance eventually grew muted and largely rhetorical (Somchai 2006, pp. 38– 52). Thailand's more than a million speakers of Northern Khmer, who are the major linguistic and identity group in Surin, Srisaket, and Buriram provinces, maintain such a low and subordinated profile as to be virtually invisible (Vail 2007). Muslims in Bangkok and in most of Thailand have accepted the hybridized status of 'Thai Muslims', Muslims whose 'Muslim-ness' is incorporated into a broader Thai identity, which in no way threatens or criticizes the dominant group, discourse, and ideology of the nation. But Malay Muslims in the Southern border provinces offer a resistance to the hegemonic discourse of Thai-ness that clearly distinguishes Malay Muslims from all other groups in Thailand. As Jory has argued, in response, the Thai state has simply refused to recognize their distinctiveness, placing them instead within the lumpen category of 'Thai Muslims': 'within official discourse of Thai-ness while there is a place for Muslims, it seems there is no place for Malays' (Jory 2006, p. 43).

Managing the Malays

In recent decades, the Thai state has used a combination of approaches to address the issue. Leeway granting was the primary theme of the post-1980s elite pact through which the South was managed, as a result of actions by the Prem Tinsulanond governments of 1980 to 1988. A central plank of this approach was the creation of certain special governance and consultative arrangements symbolized by the establishment of the Southern Border Provinces Administrative Centre (SBPAC).

At the same time, leeway granting went hand-in-hand with minority management. While Malay Muslim elites were allowed to benefit from the ownership of private Islamic schools, and to enter a wide range of political roles including those of MP and minister, this granting of leeway did not mean a real diminution of Thai suspicions regarding Malay 'loyalty'. When political violence in the deep South re-emerged in 2004, elements of the Thai state were quick to blame the very same Malay Muslim elites who had been their closest collaborators. Wadah group politicians (who then formed part of the government Thai Rak Thai Party) were widely believed by the Thai security forces to be behind the violence. One Wadah MP, Najmuddin Umar, was actually charged with treason by the Thai authorities, though the charges were later dropped (Prasert 2009). Especially after 2004, the military engaged in close scrutiny of local elites, who were subjected to regular visits, interviews, and various forms of harassment. Despite an apparent willingness to cut Malay Muslims some slack, the Thai state ultimately harboured deep misgivings about the trustworthiness and reliability even of those it had selected as its primary operatives in the community. Wherever granted, leeway needed to be policed, monitored, and tightly managed.

An alternative approach to the problem was to redefine the nature of the relationship between Bangkok and the deep South with reference to a new doctrine of multiculturalism. Such a doctrine was laid out by former Prime Minister Anand Panyarachun, who chaired the 2005–06 National Reconciliation Commission (NRC) to examine possible solutions to the Southern Thai conflict. In a televised conversation with then Prime Minister Thaksin Shinawatra in July 2005, Anand pointed out that Thailand was characterized by considerable ethnic and cultural diversity: Thaksin was of Chinese descent, and he himself had Mon origins. He argued that embracing and celebrating this diversity would create a more comfortable space for Malay Muslims within Thai society.[5] While the NRC's political proposals for addressing the violence were very modest – and widely criticized – Anand's most distinctive achievement was to shift the discourse towards models of multiculturalism, itself a significant change.

In a September 2005 speech, Anand took the argument a stage further. There he argued that Thais had lost many of their traditional values, including notions of 'sufficiency economy' (an important royal theme) and self-help (Anand 2005, p. 16). By contrast, Malay Muslim villages often lived very simple lives that were close to such values, since they 'don't aspire to use more money than necessary, they have a sense of satisfaction in sufficiency, they are not attached to consumer culture' (p. 16). In other words, Malay Muslims could be more Thai than the Thai, offering a potential 'way back' to Thai-ness for those who had lost sight of their original identity. Anand's view implied a romanticization of the village and 'traditional' self-help culture framed by royalist ideas of the sufficiency economy. This was a radical, indeed quite an extraordinary, claim which could be evaluated in different ways: as an excess of political correctness, or as a remarkable critical insight. Anand's support for ideas of multiculturalism – always subtly tied to quasi-essentialist notions of Thai-ness – represented an emerging theme for 'royal liberalism' (see Connors 2008, 2009a), a stance adopted by leading actors closely affiliated with Thailand's influential monarchy. Nonetheless, as Michael Connors has argued, it was a shift nestled within historical changes that had taken place in

Thailand over more than twenty years, and reflected the gradual rise of cultural diversity discourses (Connors 2009b). In effect, Anand advanced multiculturalism as a re-totalizing discourse to replace hard-line Thai nationalism, offering a new seating plan for the country's various minority populations. Ultimately, however, Anand's Thai-style multiculturalism was a top-down paternalistic project based on an expanded concept of Thai-ness. It did not amount to a real acknowledgement of difference, but was more a quest for the lowest common denominator and enlarged shared ground. As Connors (2009b) has argued, 'Thai-ness cannot escape its origins as an ethno-ideology, and while subordinate identities can flourish under it, none can stand equal to it' (p. 113).

Subjects, citizens, or what?

In theory, Thais are citizens with rights based on successive constitutions. The 1997 and 2007 constitutions, for example, offer detailed specification concerning citizen rights. However, in practice, the nature of the Thai monarchy perpetuates a sense of subjecthood amongst Thais. Contrary to some claims, Thailand does not have a constitutional monarchy, but an extra-constitutional monarchy in which the palace – which may include royal advisors, courtiers, and an extended network of those who invoke their loyalty to the monarchy – enjoys considerable informal, unspoken, and unwritten authority. In other words, understanding the nature of power and social relations in Thailand involves moving beyond purely legal notions and engaging with more complex, ambiguous, and non-formal realities. I will argue here that this approach involves critically unpacking legalistic understandings of citizenship and engaging with notions of 'informal citizenship'. In other words, being a citizen of a country such as Thailand is not an either/or matter, but a question of degree. All Thai people may be citizens, but some Thai people are more 'citizenly' than others. While the legally-constituted graduated citizenship experienced by Thailand's Chinese minority in the 1950s may be a thing of the past, informally-graduated citizenship is a persistent reality, especially for Thailand's Malay Muslims. Malay Muslims have not been exempted from conscription because of fears about their disloyalty – as the Chinese were between 1953 and 1956 – but under an informal policy, conscripts from the Southern border provinces were deployed only in other regions of Thailand.[6]

For those living in western countries, citizenship may seem a relatively uncomplicated issue, but for many millions of people in Southeast Asia, citizenship is fraught with ambiguity and complexity. As Stefan Ehrentraut has argued (Ehrentraut 2009), Cambodians operate on a continuum of citizenship categories, compounded by the lack of proper census data and birth registrations: some genuine citizens have genuine citizenship papers or ID cards; some genuine citizens have fake papers; and many fake citizens have fake papers. Those without proper papers may be subject to harassment, may need to pay bribes, and may be extremely vulnerable to changing regimes of regulation or simply to the transfer of individual officials between posts. Similar concerns apply in respect of many ethnic minority groups in Northern Thailand, including hundreds of thousands of 'stateless' Karen, as well as to huge swathes of the Burmese population. For such people, citizenship is always a question of negotiation. Even Thailand's most liberal constitution (that of 1997) explicitly assigned rights only to citizens: non-citizens had no constitutional rights.

The political theorist David Beetham has distinguished between 'procedural' and 'substantive' forms of democracy: procedural democracy is all about elections and parliaments, while substantive democracy involves questions of representation and participation (Beetham 1991). I would suggest that citizenship, like democracy, is a concept that operates on multiple levels. In Thailand, it is possible to hold procedural citizenship without substantive citizenship, since full citizenship contains informal elements that are unspoken, and yet are implicitly understood by everyone. Those who hold Thai nationality but do not participate in shared notions of Thai-ness are merely 'formal' or 'paper' citizens. Full Thai citizenship means holding formal citizenship plus embracing Thai-ness. It also means that those who do not feel entirely Thai should suffer from at least a mild form of Thai deficiency syndrome. In other words, we may provisionally distinguish between three categories of Thai citizen: full citizens who feel completely Thai; formal citizens who suffer from Thai deficiency syndrome; and paper citizens who do not suffer from Thai deficiency syndrome.

In the end, Thai-ness trumps Thai nationality (Thongchai 1994). Some non-Thais successfully 'pass' as Thai, because they speak Thai without an accent, and display outward adherence to the basic principles of Thai identity. 'Real' Thai citizens are supposed to subscribe to shared notions of identity, based on a loyalty to the three-part shibboleth 'Nation, Religion, King'. 'Nation' here implies the Thai nation as constructed during the reign of King Chulalongkorn: a centralized, unitary state subordinated to the power of Bangkok, in which all subsidiary identities are suppressed. This is problematic for many Malay Muslims, who regard their incorporation into Siam (later Thailand) as recent, arbitrary, and rather unwelcome. Many look back nostalgically to the earlier period of an independent or quasi-independent Patani state, with its own proud traditions as a centre of Islamic learning. 'Religion' actually means Buddhism, the *de facto* state religion. Non-Buddhists can share Thai identity only insofar as they are willing to accommodate themselves to the dominance of Buddhism, to refrain from proselytizing, and to moderate their self-presentation and their religious demands. Of the three words, though, 'King' is the most important. Full Thai citizens are supposed both to feel and to express their unquestioning loyalty to the monarchy. Again, this is a difficult proposition for Malay Muslims living in Thailand. Patani had its own local kings (and, at one time, queens) who were co-opted, incorporated, and suppressed by the Siamese. While most Malay Muslims accept the Thai monarchy, few look upon it with unalloyed warmth. During the June 2006 celebrations of King Bhumibol's sixtieth year on the throne, Thais all over the country donned yellow shirts, wristbands, and other garb – except for Malay Muslims. In Pattani, Yala, and Narathiwat, with a few exceptions, only government officials and Buddhists wore yellow. Apart from adherence to the notions of 'Nation, Religion, and King', Thai-ness also implies a deep attachment to the Thai language. While most Malay Muslims, especially those under forty, have at least a decent command of Thai (virtually everyone watches Thai television), for many, Thai remains a second language, acquired for pragmatic purposes, but not a core element of their identity (Madmarn 1999, p. 75). To possess Thai-ness, fluency in Thai is not sufficient: Thai should be one's mother tongue, one's language of first choice. A poor Thai accent should be a mark of shame, rather than, as some Malay Muslims still regard it, a badge of honour.[7]

'Thai-ness', the informal notion which looms larger than formal legal categories such as citizenship, is essentially incompatible with the 'Malay-ness' which defines identity for the denizens of Patani. Both Thai-ness and Malay-ness are essentialist notions of identity, rooted in mythical understandings and unable to share space on equal terms. While Kasian has asked publicly why it could not be possible to be both Malay and Thai at the same time – just as it is possible to be both Chinese and Thai at the same time – the answer is clear (Tejapira 2005).[8] The Chinese in Thailand have been willing to subordinate their Chinese-ness to Thai-ness, because they saw themselves as immigrants who needed to adapt to the rules and mores of Thai society, and because they suffered from Thai deficiency syndrome. The Malays view themselves as an indigenous people who have been colonized, are immune to Thai deficiency syndrome, and so are unwilling to play second identity fiddle to Thai-ness. Becoming Thai is actually a dual-track process: one track concerns formal citizenship recognition, which has not been a problem for Malay Muslims in the Deep South; a second track concerns informal citizenship recognition, which Malay Muslims have not even sought, let alone been granted.

A second difference between Chinese-ness and Malay-ness is that the recent re-legitimation of *lukjin* identity follows an earlier period of repression. For many decades, the Chinese (labelled the 'Jews of the East' by King Rama VI) were obliged to adopt Thai names, banned from entering government service, and forced to kowtow to their Thai 'betters'. Only after they had convincingly proven their loyalty were the Chinese granted full legal citizenship rights, and their participation in Thai-ness was acknowledged and credited. A period of marginalization, holding a provisional status as sojourners and interlopers, was virtually a pre-requisite for acceptance and approval. Approval was supported by the growing economic prosperity of China since 1979, as well as the warm diplomatic and trade relations between the two countries.

Yet, in the end, such acceptance and approval was on offer to those who would agree to play the game on Thai rules: the Sino-Thai were in a far better situation than the Chinese in Indonesia or Malaysia, for example, who have lived with historical burdens of formally unequal differentiated citizenship. Malay Muslims, who saw themselves as settled, even 'original' inhabitants of an historic homeland, were unwilling to collude with their own marginalization. In short, there are two major reasons why you cannot be Thai and Malay at the same time. First, Thais are not willing to grant Malay-ness the status of a distinct identity, not even a subordinated one.[9] Second, Malays are not willing to accept the dominance of Thai-ness, and since they feel no deficiency in themselves, they fail to express deference to Thai identity.

Obstacles to Recognizing Difference

Thai Buddhist views of the Malay-Muslim minority form a crucial element of the problem. While the majority population typically accuses Malay Muslims of harbouring 'separatist' tendencies, the exclusionary attitude of Bangkok Thais towards this group has the effect of creating a considerable degree of psychological separation, one which is compounded by the location of Pattani, Yala, and Narathiwat at the southern extremity of Thailand. Most Thai Buddhists have no reason to travel to the Malay-majority provinces and, indeed, would not dream of doing so. Thai Buddhist designations of Malay Muslims as the 'other' constitute a form of implicit separatism.

In a classic distinction made by Suhrke (1975), Thais tend to classify Malay Muslims into two contrasting groups: loyalists and separatists. In effect, Muslims are viewed in stark, binary, and highly moralistic terms: good Muslims versus bad Muslims. Good Muslims are happy with Thai 'virtuous rule', and are loyal to the benevolence of the monarchy, reflected in the justice system, the bureaucracy, and the security forces. Bad Muslims are untrustworthy, disloyal, and may be tacitly or actively supportive of separatism. Thai Buddhists tend to classify anyone seeking greater political participation for Malay Muslims as 'separatists', making little distinction between decentralization, devolution, autonomy, and outright independence. 'Separatism', literally a desire to tear apart the land and create a distinct Malay state, has been the central accusation of disloyalty made by Buddhists against Malay Muslims, a catch-all term covering a wide range of political positions. For Thai Buddhists, Malay Muslims are excessively attached to their own language, their traditional system of Islamic education (a major fount of disloyalty), and, of course, to their religion.

Conclusion

Historically, Malay Muslims in Thailand have been construed and constructed as subjects rather then citizens. Their loyalty to the monarchy has been consistently questioned and contested by the authorities, and they have been forced repeatedly to demonstrate their worthiness and their right to be considered Thai. Being Thai involves a willingness to subsume your ethnicity, language, and religious identity to a dominant discourse and mindset of Thai-ness. Malay Muslims fail to pass this basic test, and thus are 'not Thai', despite the fact that they are born in Thailand, hold Thai citizenship, and increasingly speak Thai as a first language. Given Malay Muslim ambivalence towards 'Thai-ness' (a deep unease concerning Thai society's attitudes to sexual promiscuity and drinking alcohol, for example), proving loyalty and demonstrating a willingness to embrace wider social norms is near impossible for most Malay Muslims. In their rejection of Thai-ness, Malay Muslims constitute the main site of resistance to Bangkok's political and cultural authority. They are left with an empty choice between 'separatism' and 'loyalty', one which for most of them has no meaning (Cornish 1997, p. 113). Informal notions of Thai-ness trump formal citizenship criteria and illustrate both a basic lack of modernity and the irrelevance of legalism. Malay claims offer a way forward to reconstruct ethno-nationalist notions of Thai identity.

The refusal of Malay Muslims to embrace Thai-ness is deeply subversive to the Thai state, since it contains the potential to begin unravelling the paternalistic nature of relations between the Thai state and its subjects/citizens. Malay Muslim demands for control over their own political resources represent a profound challenge to Thai self-colonization and deep-rooted paternalism. It is for this reason that even progressive, liberal elites have tried to play down arguments for autonomy and decentralization. For a minority in Thailand to assert its distinctive identity is to demonstrate disloyalty and is readily constructed as a prelude to overt rebellion. This is even more so when, as with Malay Muslims, that identity is linked to demands for political authority and power. Thai citizenship does not accord rights of active political participation to members of self-proclaimed minorities; such rights belong only to those who have warmly embraced Thai-ness, and are indeed the primary preserve of Bangkokians.

In the face of an ongoing violent conflict, Malay Muslims remain structurally marginalized. Two major alternatives to the status quo have emerged. One is that Thai society adopts notions of multiculturalism and becomes much less suspicious of Malays and other minorities. In other words, more leeway is granted, without the usual accompanying emphasis on micro-managing minorities and especially monitoring the Malay Muslim elite for the slightest sign of imagined disloyalties. A second alternative is that the Thai state proceeds with some form of substantive decentralization, transferring major responsibilities for governing the deep South to Malay Muslims. Schwarzmantel (2003) has argued, as a general proposition, that the global decline of homogeneity can only be addressed through solutions based on devolution and forms of autonomy (Schwarzmantel 2003, p. 108). Both of these alternatives would mark a complete break with the old models of nation-building and identity suppression that have characterized Thai approaches to ethnic minorities until now. Both routes would involve a more flexible notion of citizenship which would extend informal citizenship to Malay Muslims, over and above the formal, paper citizenship they currently hold. Both routes may have to await a new political order, perhaps in a new reign, before they can be readily pursued. A 'culturally intermediate Malay-Thai community', parallel to the 'culturally intermediate Sino-Thai community' identified by Kasian, has yet to emerge convincingly in the deep South of Thailand.

The Southern Thai case highlights the inadequacy of most recent writing about the subject of citizenship. As Sassen (2006) has argued, we need to develop a more sophisticated grasp of the available variants of formal and informal citizenship (Sassen 2006, p. 203). I have argued here that citizenship, like democracy, is not an either/or, but a matter of degree. Only by understanding citizenship as a continuum can we hope accurately to capture and to analyse how ethnic and religious minorities negotiate their relationships with the state. For much of the world's population, the status, rights, and above all the identity of the citizen remains intensely contingent and contested.

Acknowledgements

The author gratefully acknowledges funding from the Economic and Social Research Council, grant number RES-000-22-134.

Notes

1.   The new Chularajamontri appointed in 2010 is a Southerner, but from Songkhla rather than the Malay-majority region.
2.   Interview with academic, 6 January 2006.
3.   Interview 3 March 2006.
4.   I owe this phrase and some of these ideas to a very useful personal communication from Michael Montesano, 15 April 2010.
5.   'Kansanthana phiset ruang kansang santhisuk nai 3 jangwat chaidaen phaktai', [Special conversation about peace-building in the three Southern border provinces], broadcast at 20.35 on 28 July 2005, on TV Channel 11.
6.   Interview with Thai military correspondent, 16 April 2006.
7.   Exceptions are made here for half-Westerner-half-Thais (*lukkrung*); and for celebrities of ambiguous ethnicity, such as former Miss Universe Pornthip Nakhirunkanok and golfer Tiger Woods, who are viewed as Thai because of their status and achievements, despite their lack of fluency in the language. For a relevant discussion, see Callahan 1998.
8.   When Kasian raised the comparison between the Chinese and the Malays at a Hat Yai conference in 2005, he was criticized by a prominent Malay-Muslim politician for failing to distinguish between an indigenous and an immigrant minority.
9.   An Interior Ministry document issued for the guidance of Thai government officials in the region actually banned them from referring to Malay Muslims as 'Malay', on the grounds that the term might 'create dissatisfaction' or 'create division' (Connors 2009, p. 121).

References

ANAND, PANYARACHUN 2005 'Kansangkhwam samanachan lae feunfu thongthin phak tai', ['Building reconciliation and restoring locality in the South'], Keynote address, *Proceedings of the Regional Meeting of the Political Science and Public Administration Association (Southern region)*, 29 September 2005, Hat Yai: Department of Public Administration, Prince of Songkhla University
ASKEW, MARC 2008 'Thailand's intractable Southern war: policy, insurgency and discourse', *Contemporary Southeast Asia*, vol. 30, no. 2, pp. 186–214
BARNARD, TIMOTHY (ed.) 2004 *Contesting Malayness: Malay Identity Across Boundaries*, Singapore: Singapore University Press
BEETHAM, DAVID 1991 *The Legitimation of Power*, Basingstoke: Macmillan
CALLAHAN, WILLIAM A 1998 'The ideology of Miss Thailand in national, consumerist and transnational space', *Alternatives*, vol. 23, no. 1, pp. 29–62
—— 2003 'Beyond cosmopolitanism and nationalism: diasporic Chinese and neo-nationalism in China and Thailand', *International Organization*, vol. 57, no. 3, pp. 481–517
CONNORS, MICHAEL K. 2007 *Democracy and National Identity in Thailand*, 2nd edn, Copenhagen: NIAS
—— 'Article of faith: the failure of *royal liberalism* in Thailand', *Journal of Contemporary Asia*, vol. 38, no. 1, pp.143–65
—— 2009a 'Liberalism, authoritarianism and the politics of decisionism in Thailand', *Pacific Review*, vol. 22, no. 3, pp. 355–73
—— 2009b 'Another country: reflections on the politics and culture of the Muslim South', in John Funston (ed.), *Divided Over Thaksin: Thailand's Coup and Problematic Transition*, Singapore: ISEAS, pp. 112–3
CORNISH, ANDREW 1997 *Whose Place is This? Malay Rubber Producers and Thai Government Officials in Yala*, Bangkok: White Lotus
COUGHLIN, R. J. 1960 *Double Identity: The Chinese in Modern Thailand*, Hong Kong: Hong Kong University Press

EHRENTRAUT, STEFAN 2009 'Perpetually temporary: citizenship and ethnic Vietnamese in Cambodia', *Ethnic and Racial Studies*, DOI: 10.1080/01419870.2010.537359

INTERNATIONAL CRISIS GROUP 2005 *Southern Thailand: Insurgency, not Jihad. Asia Report 98*, May 2005, http://www.crisisgroup.org (accessed 19 October 2009)

JORY, PATRICK 2006 'From "Patani Melayu" to "Thai Muslim"', *ISIM Review*, Autumn, vol. 18, pp. 42–3

KABEER, NAILA (ed.) 2005 *Inclusive Citizenship: Meanings and Expressions*, London: Zed

KASIAN, TEJAPIRA 1992 'Pigtail: a pre-history of Chineseness in Thailand', *SOJOURN*, vol. 7, no. 2, pp. 95–122

—— 2005 *Jek lae khaek kap sangkhom thai: phinit panha thai musalim chuasai malayu jak prasobkan khonthai chuasai chin* [Jeks and khaeks: analysis of the problem of Thai Muslims of Malay ethnicity from the experience of a Thai of Chinese ethnicity], paper presented 8 December at Taksin University, Songkhla

—— 2009 'The misbehaving jeks: the evolving regime of Thai-ness and Sino-Thai challenges', *Asian Ethnicity*, vol. 10, no. 2, pp. 263–83

KYMLICKA, WILL and NORMAN, WAYNE 1995 'Return of the citizen: a survey of recent work on citizenship theory', in Ronald Beiner (ed.), *Theorising Citizenship*, Albany NY: SUNY Press

MCCARGO, DUNCAN 2008 *Tearing Apart the Land: Islam and Legitimacy in Southern Thailand*, Ithaca NY: Cornell University Press

—— 2010, 'Co-optation and resistance in Thailand's Muslim South: the changing role of Islamic council elections', *Government and Opposition*, vol. 45, no. 1, pp. 93–113

MADMARN, HASAN 1999 *The Pondok and Madrasah in Patani*, Bangi: UKM Press

MARSHALL, T. H. 1950 *Citizenship and Social Class and Other Essays*, Cambridge: Cambridge University Press

MILLER, TOBY 2002 'Cultural citizenship', in Engin F. Isin and Bryan S. Turner (eds), *Handbook of Citizenship Studies*, London: Sage, pp. 231–43

MOHAMAD, MAHATHIR BIN 1970 *The Malay Dilemma*, Singapore: Times Books

MONTESANO, MICHAEL and JORY, PATRICK (eds) 2008, *Thai South and Malay North: Ethnic Interactions on a Plural Peninsula*, Singapore: NUS Press

NAREERAT, PARISUTHIWUTTIPORN 2000 'Role of Chinese in Mahasarakham: municipal to local politics', seminar paper

PRASERT, CHAITHONGPAN 2009 *Khaoha wa (so so Najmuddin) ben kabot* [*Accusation of Treason (against MP Najmuddin)*], Bangkok: Saiyaiprachatham Publishing

SASSEN, SASKIA 2006 'The repositioning of citizenship and alienage: emergent subjects and spaces for politics', in Kate E. Tunstall (ed.), *Displacement, Asylum, Migration*, Oxford: Oxford University Press, pp. 176–203

SATHA-ANAND, CHAIWAT (ed.) 2009 *Imagined Land: The State and Southern Violence in Thailand*, Fuchu: ILCAA, Tokyo University of Foreign Languages

SCHWARZMANTEL, JOHN 2003 *Citizenship and Identity: Towards a New Republic*, London: Routledge

SOMCHAI, PHATHARATHANANUNTH 2006 *Civil Society and Democratization: Social Movements in Northeast Thailand*, Copenhagen: NIAS

SUHRKE, ASTRI 1975 'Irredentism contained: the Thai-Muslim case', *Comparative Politics*, vol. 7, no. 2, pp. 187–203

SUJIT WONGTHES 1987 Jek Bon Lao (Chinese on Top of Lao), *Sinlapa Wattanatham* (*Art and Culture Magazine*) special issue

TAN, MICHELLE Forthcoming 'Symbiosis and subordination: politicising Sino-Thai ethnicity', *Critical Asian Studies*

THONGCHAI, WINICHAKUL 1994 *Siam Mapped: A History of the Geo-Body of a Nation*, Honolulu HI: University of Hawai'i Press

TURNER, BRYAN S. 2001 'The erosion of citizenship', *British Journal of Sociology*, vol. 52, no. 2, pp. 189–209

VAIL, PETER 2007 'Thailand's Khmer as "invisible minority": language, ethnicity and cultural politics in north-eastern Thailand', *Asian Ethnicity*, vol. 8, no. 2, pp. 111–30

YOUNG, IRIS MARION 1989 'Polity and group difference: a critique of the ideal of universal citizenship', *Ethics*, vol. 99, pp. 250–74

YUSUF, IMTIAZ 2010 'The role of the *Chularajamontri (Shaykh al-Islam)* in resolving ethno-religious conflict in Southern Thailand', *American Journal of Islamic Social Sciences*, vol. 27, no. 1, pp. 31–53

'Indigenous peoples' rights' as a strategy of ethnic accommodation: contrasting experiences of Cordillerans and Papuans in the Philippines and Indonesia

Jacques Bertrand

Abstract

In Southeast Asia, the use of 'indigenous peoples' as a category for ethnic accommodation has had mixed results. Cordillerans and Papuans pursued dual strategies, sometimes casting themselves as 'nations', other times as 'indigenous peoples'. While Cordillerans obtained rights as indigenous peoples, Papuans failed. Both obtained concessions during constitutional talks but only Cordillerans obtained recognition and rights as indigenous peoples. Cordillerans used linkages to the international indigenous rights movement and successfully lobbied the Constitutional Commission; electoral incentives were also key to the adoption of subsequent legislation. Conversely, Papuans were given concessions but not rights as indigenous peoples because, along with other indigenous groups, they were closed off from constitutional reform talks and lacked a strong network to put pressure on the state. This article shows that domestic coalitions in conjunction with the international indigenous rights movement might only succeed through effective framing during critical junctures of constitutional change when states are vulnerable.

States respond in varied ways to demands for indigenous peoples' rights, by denying their existence, repression, or conversely, by accommodation. At the same time, such demands have been growing as the international indigenous rights movement constructed a category of 'indigenous peoples' that is applied to a whole range of different groups.

In Asia, many states long rejected the existence of indigenous peoples and corresponding rights. Yet, in the last couple of decades some, such as the Philippines, have changed course quite significantly. Indigenous peoples in the Philippines now benefit from recognized status that is constitutionalized and from rights that are specified in legislation. While its implementation and realized benefits can be criticized, nevertheless such legal recognition provides for defenders of indigenous peoples' rights a benchmark against which to hold the government accountable.

This article addresses the processes involved in such a shift in policy. Specifically, it focuses on Cordillerans in the Philippines, and Papuans in Indonesia: two groups that had similar conditions, that engaged states with similar kinds of ethnic diversity, and that could choose to advocate for indigenous peoples' rights or seek autonomy as 'nations'. Both Cordillerans and Papuans attempted to build bridges across smaller constituent groups that made up their broader, constructed, 'pan-identity' (Finin 2005). Cordillerans constitute a loose constellation of the various tribal groups that inhabit the mountainous Cordillera region of Northern Luzon in the Philippines. 'Papuan' is an umbrella identity that was constructed out of the numerous smaller groups of the western half of the island of New Guinea. Originally occupied by the Dutch, the territory was ceded to Indonesia in 1963, and has been officially a province of Indonesia since 1969.

Both groups used similar strategies to advance their interests. They cast themselves in some forums as 'nations', and in others as 'indigenous peoples'. As nations, they pursed regional autonomy and differentiated status from other groups. As 'indigenous peoples', they created alliances with other self-identified 'indigenous' groups to put pressure on the state for recognition and rights. Cordillerans, for instance, created linkages to the 'Lumad' of Mindanao, while Papuans joined the large number of smaller groups in Indonesia that eventually joined the Alliance of Indigenous Peoples of the Archipelago (Aliansi Masyarakat Adat Nusantara, or AMAN). Finally, both groups used violence that, in combination with their active engagement in international forums, sustained the state's attention.

Yet, Cordillerans were successful in obtaining recognition and rights as indigenous peoples, while Papuans failed. The Philippines enshrined indigenous peoples' rights in its 1987 constitution,[1] and in 1997 adopted path-breaking legislation, the Indigenous Peoples' Rights Act (IPRA). The Indonesian government neither recognized nor legislated in favour of indigenous peoples. Why?

I offer an explanation in two parts. The state's decision to accommodate an ethnic group and extend some form of differentiated status is separate from the character of this accommodation. After years of repressing or ignoring group claims, the decision to shift policy requires in itself an explanation but it does not imply any specific set of policies. I treat separately the decision to extend rights as indigenous peoples (as opposed to national minority for instance). The Philippine and Indonesian states made concessions respectively to Cordillerans and Papuans at critical junctures of state vulnerability. But Cordillerans obtained recognition and, later, favourable legislation because they were highly successful at tapping the international indigenous rights movement and then lobbying the Constitutional Commission to enshrine recognition and rights for indigenous peoples; electoral incentives were also key to the adoption of subsequent legislation.

Conversely, the Indonesian government faced little pressure from the weak indigenous peoples' movement. Yet, it extended concessions to Papuans because it faced even more threatening claims in other parts of the country, such as East Timor and Aceh where conflict had been much more violent and intense. Oddly enough, recognizing indigenous peoples' rights would have been much less risky than giving autonomy to Papuans, which could feed further demands for secession. Papuans played the 'indigenous' card ambiguously, as they also maintained demands as a nation (Mote and Rutherford 2001; Webster 2002; Chauvel 2005). Despite AMAN's recent creation, no strong network of indigenous peoples was present at the time of crucial changes in the constitution, whereas autonomy had been floated as a solution to the country's problems in East Timor, Aceh, and Papua, and was constitutionalized instead. Once this path was set, it virtually closed off options to articulate and obtain claims as 'indigenous'.

More broadly, the comparison between Cordillerans and Papuans points to the importance of critical junctures, state vulnerability, and the articulation of indigenous identities at crucial moments of constitutional making. At a time of regime change in particular, ongoing insurgency or threats to political stability create intense pressure for political resolution. Such vulnerability creates a structural precondition for accommodation but in the process of amending the constitutional order or modifying institutional structures, the range of its possible forms is often wide. A well-organized domestic coalition can offer a strong rationale for one type of recognition and set of rights over another. The comparison of Cordillerans and Papuans suggests that, although the international indigenous rights movement in conjunction with domestic coalitions can exert pressure on states, effective framing during critical junctures might be the only opportunity to change state policy. Once constitutionalized, indigenous peoples' rights became part of the electoral landscape and a benchmark for seeking further legislation, which was then infused with influence from the international movement for indigenous peoples' rights.

International lobbying, domestic pressure, and state resistance

Cordillerans and Papuans first mobilized against authoritarian regimes that generally repressed demands for ethnic recognition and accommodation. They used various strategies – including violent mobilization, international alliances, and domestic coalitions – to pressurize their respective states. They also strategically shifted how they framed their grievances, sometimes articulating a claim as 'nation' and other times as 'indigenous peoples'. Both states were generally averse to any ethnic accommodation. Furthermore, efforts to gain recognition as 'indigenous peoples' was particularly difficult in the Asian context because of the absence of a clear distinction between 'indigenous' and 'non-indigenous' groups.

Indonesia and the Philippines are similarly diverse, ethnically and linguistically. Almost all groups have long inhabited their territory, with very little record of their origins. Only Chinese and perhaps Arabs in Indonesia could be identified as later migrants. Colonial occupation did not significantly alter this demographic landscape. At independence, both states pursued various strategies to maintain unity but regional and ethnic distinctions remained strong (Kahin 1955). The sharp distinction in the histories of indigenous peoples in other areas of the world was not reproduced in these countries. At most, some groups were more isolated and less in contact with colonial authorities or post-independence state bureaucracies.

At the international level, Asian states long resisted the distinction between indigenous and non-indigenous, claiming either that all inhabitants were indigenous or none were present in their land (Barnes, Andrew and Kingsbury 1995, p. 2). They did so against the backdrop of remarkable changes at the international level. First formally recognized in ILO conventions 107 (1957) and 169 (1989), the indigenous peoples' movement only really took off after it entered the UN system in the 1980s and 1990s.

At its origins, indigenous peoples' rights became part of the international agenda after mobilization in the Americas. By 1977, the international network was launched when representatives from more than sixty indigenous groups met in the International NGO conference on Discrimination against Indigenous Populations (Niezen 2003, pp. 40–4). In the early 1980s, the newly created UN Working Group on Indigenous Populations (WGIP), under the United Nations High Commissioner for Human Rights, became a unique platform for groups to gain international profile. With a principle of broad inclusion, the WGIP and the indigenous peoples' movement grew considerably in the following decade, reaching even eight hundred groups represented in the 2001 WGIP meetings (Niezen 2003, pp. 45–6; Morgan 2007, pp. 276–82).

Self-identification as 'indigenous' became an accepted standard to attend these international forums and later to claim rights. One of the most used definitions of indigenous peoples, by Martínez Cobo, emphasizes self-definition, historical continuity with a pre-colonial or pre-invasion past, non-dominance, ancestral territories, and ethnic identity (Kingsbury 1995, p. 26).[2] Self-identification recognized the impossibility of finding any objective basis for making distinctions between 'indigenous' and 'non-indigenous', and emphasized instead the political construction of the identity. In Asian countries, the category of 'indigenous' peoples was particularly problematic because of its connotation of prior occupancy. States such as Indonesia and the Philippines denied the existence of indigenous peoples in their countries on the basis that they were all indigenous (Sanders 1989, pp. 416–17; Kingsbury 1999; Howard 2003, p. 144).

The WGIP's main focus was the drafting of the UN Declaration on the Rights of Indigenous Peoples. Most of the draft was essentially written between 1985 and 1993 but encountered strong resistance from many states that prevented it from being finalized. Its central achievement included Article 3, which spelled out a right to self-determination. It was also its main stumbling block as states continued to fear that it could amount to allowing secessionism (Hyndman 1991; Daes 2000; Morgan 2004). Continued lobbying and campaigns to advance indigenous peoples' rights eventually led to a breakthrough and in September 2007 the General Assembly adopted the UN Declaration on the Rights of Indigenous Peoples, of which most Asian states became signatories.

Cordillerans and Papuans began to use international forums in the 1980s in the hope of creating some pressure on their respective governments, first as nations and later as 'indigenous peoples'. They were not alone, of course, in seeking international support to advance minority rights in the Philippines and Indonesia. In the Philippines, the Moro National Liberation Front, and later the Moro Islamic Liberation Front, waged a guerilla war against the Philippine state (McKenna 1998). In Indonesia, the Free Aceh Movement (Gerakan Aceh Merdeka, or GAM) had risen against the Suharto regime in 1976 but was swiftly crushed (Morris 1985; Aspinall 2009). In East Timor, Fretilin and Falintil, its armed wing, used insurgency and diplomacy to seek independence from Indonesia. East Timorese and Acehnese sought their own state or wide-ranging autonomy within Indonesia (Bertrand and Laliberté 2010).

Cordillerans and Papuans, however, followed dual strategies. Cordillerans first pursued armed struggle as a sub-state nation, initially in conjunction with the communist New People's Army (NPA). Papuans also made international appeals as a sub-state nation. In international forums, they appealed to the right of self-determination of nations, arguing that they had been forcibly integrated into Indonesia. They considered undemocratic the UN-sanctioned Act of Free Choice of 1969 that involved handpicked representatives under repressive conditions. In the 1980s, however, Papuans also began to attend international forums on indigenous peoples' rights. Cordillerans mostly espoused this new strategy, while Papuans pursued multiple fronts and approaches.

Cordillerans began to resist in the 1970s. Initially part of the NPA, Cordillerans subsequently attempted to create a Cordilleran identity as 'nation' that, in the end, was not very successful (Rood 1987; Rood 1991; Finin 2005). Instead, they saw an opportunity to tap into the discourse on indigenous rights, in particular to obtain recognition of rights to ancestral lands and self-determination. The Cordillera People's Alliance (CPA), formed in 1984, made the strategic decision to shift away from the broader objectives of the Communist movement and to cast Cordillerans as indigenous peoples (Prill-Brett 1994, pp. 693–4; Hyndman 1991, p. 173). They were one of the first groups from Asia to join the international movement and cast itself as 'indigenous'.

For the first time, Cordilleran representatives made an appearance before the UN Working Group on Indigenous Populations in 1984. They voiced grievances such as the absence of rights to ancestral domains, of rights to the utilization and management of resources on these lands, the non-recognition of the viability of their socio-political structures, the lack of adequate representation, the disrespect and non-recognition of cultural identity and integrity, as well as the militarization of their region (CWIS 1984). In subsequent years, they continued to make similar requests for support from the UN WGIP. They even came to play a leading role within the movement. Victoria Tauli-Corpuz, head of the Tebtebba foundation and closely linked to the CPA, was one of the most active indigenous leaders in the WGIP. She eventually led the UN Permanent Forum on Indigenous Issues (UNPFII).

The international engagement of Cordillerans with the indigenous peoples' movement had two effects. In combination with domestic pressure at the crucial moment of transition to democracy and state vulnerability, Cordillerans' international presence helped to access information and strategies to steer the Constitutional Commission in the direction of enshrining indigenous peoples' rights. It was difficult for the new democratic government of the Philippines to deny the existence of indigenous peoples when it sought ways to curb the ongoing insurgency and Cordillerans had positioned themselves so significantly on the international stage.

Later, the leadership role of the Cordilleran representatives at the UN level continued to create moral pressure to follow up on constitutional commitments with more concrete legislation. Although one should not exaggerate these effects, clearly the ability to maintain indigenous issues on the agenda helped to raise the stakes for adopting progressive legislation and defining a particular set of rights in line with emerging normative standards in discussions over the draft Declaration. The adoption of IPRA in 1997 can be seen as reflecting, in part, the outcome of these international pressures. In particular, its content was highly influenced by information supplied through lobbying from the Tebtebba foundation and other indigenous peoples' groups.

Papuans on the other hand, had different results. The 'Papuan' identity was constructed from an amalgamation of sub-groups scattered across a mountainous landscape. It was fostered in part by Dutch colonial authorities that sought to combat an eventual integration into Indonesia. West New Guinea had been left out of negotiations at the time of Indonesia's independence. Later, however, the Indonesian government launched a campaign to acquire it from the Dutch. Negotiations brokered by the United Nations eventually led to the cession of West New Guinea to Indonesia, and in 1969 to the Act of Free Choice that sealed its official integration with UN approval (Lijphart 1966; Chauvel 2005).

After its integration, West New Guinea, renamed Irian Jaya, was restructured to conform to Indonesia's political and administrative structure. It obtained the status of province and its territory was subdivided into regencies, districts, and villages, as specified in the Regional Law of 1974. There were no modifications made to account for the different socio-economic, political, and cultural differences that distinguished the area from the rest of Indonesia. The government imposed stringent restrictions on cultural expression through the educational system or other public fora. Indonesian was adopted as the sole language of education, and the national curriculum was readily imposed on Papuans with basically no local content (Lagerberg 1979; Tapol 1984; Defert 1996; Bertrand 2004, pp. 151–3).

The central government also controlled the management of land and natural resources. Under the Constitution of 1945, natural resources were part of the public domain and were exploited according to policies set at the centre. For instance, it promoted the establishment of the Freeport-McMoran mine, which became a frequent target of protest for its failure to benefit local Papuans.

During the 1980s, the government encouraged migration to Irian Jaya in all of its forms. From the state's perspective, Irian Jaya constituted a vast area of relatively empty lands, sparsely populated, and with vast possibilities for economic development. Moreover, it promised to relieve the stress on resources and land in other parts of the archipelago. The state therefore promoted a transmigration programme by which people from the heavily-populated island of Java were encouraged to move to Irian Jaya. The government claimed whole areas for these transmigration sites without regard to whether Papuans made any claims to ownership or access. In addition, it encouraged spontaneous migration, which grew steadily for three decades so that Papuans almost lost their majority status.

The Free Papua Movement (Organisasi Papua Merdeka, or OPM) emerged shortly after the Act of Free Choice. It sought independence through armed resistance. It never mounted a large-scale resistance, however, as it remained relatively divided and not well armed. Nevertheless, it waged small-scale attacks in defiance of Indonesian authorities, and carried the symbol of Papuans' resistance to the Indonesian state (Osborne 1985; King 2002).

Papuans were the main Indonesian group that sent representatives to the WGIP in the 1980s. In their first appearance before the WGIP, they contested the legitimacy of the Act of Free Choice and UN support for integration to Indonesia. A large emphasis was placed on disappearances and killings allegedly perpetrated by Indonesian armed forces, repression of the expression of Papuan culture, and the seizures of land for mining and transmigration sites (Free Papua Movement 1984). In subsequent years, they emphasized the devastating effects of the World Bank-sponsored transmigration programme, by which settlers from other regions of Indonesia were deemed to be forcibly occupying Papuan land owned by their 'ancestors' (CWIS 1985b).

After the fall of the authoritarian regime in 1998, Papuans increased their networking internationally, particularly in indigenous peoples' forums. Organizations such as ELSHAM (a legal aid organization) that had tapped into the international human rights network presented the Papuan case at the WGIP (ELSHAM 2003; LP3BH 2004). After 2002, the newly-created Dewan Adat Papua (Papuan Customary Council, or DAP), composed of representatives of all 253 Papuan tribal groups, assumed the leadership role in international forums (Mandowen 2005).

The Indonesian government, however, remained strongly consistent in manipulating conceptual ambiguities to deny recognition of 'indigenous' status. During the authoritarian regime led by President Suharto, the government argued that Indonesia was composed of 'many different ethnic groups, indigenous to our various regions', while upholding principles of non-discrimination and respect for all cultures in the country (CWIS 1985a). In response to a critical report on Papua before the UN Permanent Forum on Indigenous Peoples in 2004, it rejected criticism on the basis that Papuan peoples were attributed a status as indigenous peoples. The view was that 'as a matter of principle, Indonesia's 500 ethnic groups were all regarded as equally indigenous; any reference in the Forum's report was therefore irrelevant' (UN ESC 2004). It reiterated this position in its report to the United Nations Convention on the Elimination of all Forms of Racial Discrimination, submitted in 2006. Instead, it offered 'four principles used to determine one's ethnic group (*masyarakat adat*) i.e. names, languages, environment, and customs'. It mentioned new legislation that made no distinction between indigenous and other groups. Instead, it differentiated *masyarakat adat terpencil* (isolated or remote ethnic groups) from the broader category of *masyarakat adat* (UN CERD 2006, pp. 6, 17).

Adat can be translated as 'custom', 'tradition', or 'customary law'. Under Dutch colonial rule, customs and traditions were codified and associated with ethnic groups across the archipelago. Since independence, *adat* has retained this broad applicability, even if it has been transformed and often manipulated (Davidson and Henley 2007). The Indonesian government has refused to recognize a concept of 'indigenous peoples' and instead, in the 1990s, created programmes aimed specifically at 'isolated' *adat* communities, a much more restrictive category to allow for targeted, special development funds without attributing or recognizing distinct rights. These programmes were largely detrimental to these communities and provided little actual protection (Li 2000; Duncan 2004).

The Indonesian government, therefore, has been able to isolate itself from international pressures, thereby denying Papuans and other indigenous groups some of the leverage they hoped to gain in international forums. By casting all its peoples as 'indigenous', it supported the UN Declaration without recognizing its applicability within Indonesia. With its own legislation on *adat* communities, it could claim to be sensitive to customary traditions and laws, and to be providing help to vulnerable groups. As will be seen in the next section, the formation of a coalition of indigenous peoples in Indonesia attempted to connect *adat* with indigenous peoples' rights but has so far failed to gain much ground in this respect. Papuans, as a result, continued their dual strategy and made some gains as a sub-state nation but few as 'indigenous peoples'.

Democratization and divergent paths toward recognizing 'indigenous peoples'

As Cordillerans and Papuans tapped international networks for support, they also attempted to create new opportunities offered by democratizing regimes. Both the Philippines and Indonesia democratized rapidly after popular uprisings. In the Philippines, the People

Power revolution in 1986 created expectations of strong involvement from civil society groups. Although it ended up recreating the oligopolistic characteristics of the past, nevertheless for a brief time the regime was more open to civil society groups and included them in constitutional discussions. The Philippine constitution of 1987 enshrined rights for indigenous peoples and autonomy for the Cordillera. Cordillerans rejected proposed autonomy legislation several times. On the other hand, they welcomed the Philippine legislature's adoption of the landmark Indigenous Peoples' Rights Act in 1997.

Conversely, although the Indonesian authoritarian regime also succumbed under popular pressure, the 'Reformasi' movement only obtained the resignation of long-standing authoritarian leader Suharto. The new regime kept all the previous institutions and Suharto's vice president, Habibie, became the new president. Constitutional negotiations were carried out in commissions of the Peoples' Consultative Assembly (Majelis Permusyawaratan Rakyat, or MPR), which was composed of members elected and appointed during the previous authoritarian regime. The process of constitutional reforms, therefore, became much more controlled, limited, and less penetrated by civil society groups than in the Philippines. Autonomy was discussed and enshrined in principle without specifying particular regions, but there was no attempt to recognize indigenous peoples' rights. Later legislation granted special autonomy to Papuans, but its scope and implementation were limited.

The new democratic government in the Philippines was eager to find solutions to the NPA's insurgency. In addition to pursuing counter-insurgency campaigns, it sought political solutions. The Cordillera was an NPA stronghold, so concessions to Cordillerans could help to dissociate them from the broader Communist insurgency. Negotiations were opened with the Cordillera People's Liberation Army, led by Father Conrado Balweg. The CPLA allied itself with the government's counter-insurgency campaign, and later agreed to disband and join the formal political process.

Concessions went further, however, as discussions over a new constitution began. Key to the success of enshrining rights for indigenous peoples was the Cordillerans' ability to lobby the Constitutional Commission in alliance with domestic NGO coalitions. NGOs were successful at obtaining the inclusion of several key clauses in the Constitution because of their role in the People Power revolution. They gained influence for a brief period but they used the opportunity, particularly during constitutional negotiations, to place some of their favoured items on the agenda. Indigenous peoples obtained recognition and protection of rights in principle. Furthermore, the Cordillerans' involvement internationally allowed them to convince commission members that good democracy also required respect for indigenous peoples' rights, and recognition of rising international standards in this respect. The Cordillera also benefitted from the constitutional promise of autonomy for its region, which was obtained as part of negotiations with the CPLA to end their role in the insurgency.

Shortly after constitutional concessions, however, the Philippine state regained more strength. It limited the extent of its commitment to autonomy, especially with regard to control over resources and land, an important component of indigenous groups' claims to self-determination. In 1990, Congress passed an Organic Act for the creation of an autonomous region, but the CPA mobilized against it because it lacked significant devolution of power and the state would retain control over natural resources. The Act was rejected by 70 per cent in the referendum required for its ratification (Hyndman 1991, pp. 178–82). The management and recognition of ancestral lands was then assigned to the Department of Environment and Natural Resources (DENR) rather than the interim Cordillera Administrative Region, which had been set up after 1987 and which continued to operate after autonomy was rejected (Prill-Brett 1994, p. 695).

A breakthrough occurred when in 1997 the Ramos administration adopted one of the most progressive laws for indigenous peoples, the Indigenous Peoples' Rights Act (IPRA). It gave them legal measures to protect their rights to ancestral lands, exploitation of natural resources, their traditional ways of life, customs, and socio-political structures. Mining, logging, or other development projects on ancestral domains could only be pursued with the consent of indigenous communities.

Ramos' political interests were important, but continued pressure from Cordilleran groups was also effective. Ramos had launched a Social Reform Agenda to tackle poverty with a comprehensive programme. IPRA was part of the reform programme and satisfied the political constituency that Ramos had built into a winning coalition which included civil society groups. Perhaps coincidentally, IPRA was adopted in 1997 at a time when Ramos was actively seeking to amend the constitution in order to be allowed to run for a second term. Gaining strong populist support, as well as recreating the NGO coalition of the People Power revolution, was essential to such an attempt (which eventually failed). Nevertheless, it can explain the political interests involved in pushing for socially-progressive legislation. The content of IPRA, however, reflected the intense lobbying that Cordillerans had pursued in conjunction with their international role in the indigenous peoples' movement.

Of course, IPRA has not been without its limitations. Section 56, for instance, provided for the respect of property rights already allocated within ancestral domains. Under the 1995 Mining Act, the government had allocated mining rights in the Cordillera and elsewhere, which were therefore excluded from IPRA's reach. This limitation covered a good portion of ancestral lands (Stavenhagen 2004, p. 11). A number of obstacles were also raised to IPRA's proper implementation, including impediments to effective functioning of the National Commission on Indigenous Peoples (NCIP) (Castro 2000, pp. 41–5).

Papuans, on the other hand, failed to gain recognition or protection as indigenous peoples. Yet, perhaps even more than other peoples in the archipelago, the Indonesian state often portrayed Papuans as 'backward' (King 2005, p. 94), because of their isolation, their customs, and their basic livelihoods. With educational and socio-economic levels well below the Indonesian average, and their late integration to Indonesia, Papuans could be demarcated quite clearly from other ethnic groups. Given international definitions of indigenous peoples, Papuans meet the criteria at least as much as the Cordillerans in the Philippines. Nevertheless, such recognition was never granted.

Instead, and oddly enough, Papuans were granted a form of autonomy. Even though Papuans chose to present their case in international forums on indigenous peoples, they continued to mobilize as a 'nation' seeking self-determination with a clear objective of independence. The Indonesian state might have defused the latter claims, if it had recognized Papuans as indigenous peoples, and supported legislation similar to that of the Philippines. Instead, it offered 'special autonomy', which might ironically reinforce Papuan claims to nationhood even if autonomy remained narrower than the Papuan elite hoped for, and circumscribed by other measures designed to reduce its significance, such as subsequent legislation to divide the province.

Democratization might have provided opportunities to enshrine rights as indigenous peoples, as happened in the Philippines, or it could have opened possibilities to lobby for favourable constitutional changes. While such changes did occur on autonomy, no such opportunity arose on indigenous peoples.

The role of NGOs at the time of democratization marks some of the contrast. Although NGOs and civil society groups played a role in the 'Reformasi' movement, they were excluded from subsequent constitutional negotiations. The 'Reformasi' movement was cobbled together over a few months, as the Asian Financial Crisis led to rapid economic deterioration and the regime weakened under attacks of corruption. It launched sufficiently large and sustained protests to force the resignation of Suharto but the regime's institutions and the political establishment remained in place. Suharto's vice-president, Habibie, took the reins of power and instigated a progressive and relatively controlled reform process. (Liddle 1999; Aspinall 2005)

Negotiations on constitutional amendments proceeded mainly in two ad hoc commissions of the Peoples' Consultative Assembly (MPR), the highest legislative body in Indonesia. The process remained within the commissions, and involved haggling between political parties, with little public or NGO involvement in the proceedings. Consultations were held but constitutional issues were displaced in the media by more sensationalist ones, such as impeachment proceedings against President Wahid. Major political parties in the MPR, as well as representatives from the military, were strongly nationalist in terms of wanting to preserve a strong centre and protect national unity (King 2001).

Some amendments were designed in part to accommodate ethnic diversity. Provinces had long applied pressure for a new basis of regional autonomy, since the Suharto regime had been over-centralized. Commission members were willing to make some concessions largely because of ongoing conflicts in East Timor, Aceh, and Papua. Regional units (provinces and regencies) were to exercise wide-ranging autonomy in all realms except those that, by law, were specified to be within the jurisdiction of the central government. Amendments also included sections recognizing the need to respect the 'diversity of regions' in adopting laws to regulate regional administration, and creating special units for 'regional authorities that are special and distinct'. No special provisions were made, however, for East Timor, Aceh, and Papua (Constitution Indonesia 2006, art. 18, A, B). Furthermore, constitutional amendments provided for the creation of a second legislative chamber, the Regional Representative Assembly (DPD), although its powers were much more limited than originally envisioned (King 2004, p. 129).

Indigenous peoples, however, did not gain any clear recognition in these negotiations. Article 18 of the amended constitution included a statement on protecting 'traditional communities' (*masyarakat adat*) and their rights, while article 28 on human rights also upheld the rights and cultural identities of these communities. Yet, what the government understands by these communities is different from 'indigenous peoples' as recognized internationally. Furthermore, the language of the article also implied assimilationist tendencies since such rights were to be 'in accordance with societal development and the principles of the Unitary State of the Republic of Indonesia' (art. 18) and 'in accordance with the development of times and civilisations' (Constitution Indonesia 2006).

The emergence of *masyarakat adat* to signify 'indigenous peoples' is a recent attempt on the part of NGO activists to tap into the international movement. In 1999, these NGOs contributed to the

AMAN's launch. Under authoritarianism, when references to ethnicity or tribal issues were viewed suspiciously, environmental and rights advocacy NGOs were at the forefront of contesting land-grabs and displacement that denied land rights to communities in favour of state projects or corrupt land procurement (Li 2000; Davidson and Henley 2007). They took advantage of greater political space to engage in a new form of mobilization. In AMAN's first congress in March 1999, 231 'indigenous' representatives discussed a variety of issues such as the rights of indigenous peoples and the effects on their lives of large-scale mining, fishing, and plantations. Representatives from the UN Working Group on Indigenous Populations (WGIP) and members of NGOs presented international instruments available to advance indigenous peoples' issues (AMAN 1999a).

This mobilization was not without controversy. In several communities, the new politics of *adat* was used to revive certain discourses on local customs and make claims to land, particularly against migrants (Acciaioli 2001). Groups positioned themselves as 'indigenous' to access international and national networks (Li 2000). By keeping blurred the boundaries of who belongs to the category *adat*, AMAN ran the risk of encompassing a large variety of groups across the archipelago and reclaiming land and resource rights according to group identities, while ignoring transformations brought about by migration and development. Groups legitimately attempted to obtain redress for decades of land losses and resource extraction during the Suharto regime (Li 2001). The *adat* movement provided some new form of empowerment around identity issues, but it also created a political minefield.

Nevertheless, Papuans and other self-described 'indigenous peoples' in AMAN sought to gain rights through their access to international networks and through newly-established democratic channels but no significant gains were made. The broader 'Reformasi' movement was kept at the margins of the constitutional commission and groups such as AMAM gained little access.

It was certainly not easy for AMAN to put pressure on the Indonesian government. Cordillerans benefitted from mobilizing internationally at the same time as they gained a constitutional window of opportunity domestically. Constitutional amendments in Indonesia were implemented at a time when AMAN was just beginning to mobilize. In international forums the Indonesian government had been able to shield itself and, ironically, support the UN Draft Declaration on the basis of its definitional manipulation of 'indigenous'. Its continued denial to recognize indigenous peoples in Indonesia, combined with narrow rights to *adat* communities, raised difficult obstacles for AMAN.

Papuans, therefore, supported AMAN but pursued different fora as well. By strategically positioning themselves both as a separate nation and as indigenous peoples, they hoped to make gains one way or another. For instance, rather than strongly supporting AMAN, Papuans instead declared their desire for independence in a special meeting with the newly-appointed President Habibie. This strategy diluted their political efforts, since Papuans were never strongly committed to the international indigenous peoples' movement, nor were they at the forefront of AMAN. As a result, pressure on the Indonesian government was relatively weaker than pressure on the Philippine government with respect to indigenous peoples' rights.

Still, the Indonesian government gave concessions to Papuans in the form of the Special Autonomy Law of 2001. Moving beyond previously-granted autonomy to regions, the law granted a large number of new powers, new revenues from natural resource exploitation, and a Papuan People's Assembly (Majelis Rakyat Papua, or MRP) to represent Papuan interests (relative to those of migrants to the province) (Bertrand 2004). The law, however, fell short of providing any special status or rights to Papuans as indigenous peoples. Customary groups were given representation in the MRP but the legal clout of the assembly was ambiguous and mostly restricted to consultation and approval on issues related to more restricted customary rights. Papuans obtained no powers to manage migration from other islands or mining developments that threatened their livelihoods. They obtained no rights to self-determination or greater rights over land and natural resources. Their autonomy was even diluted later when the government divided the province (Bertrand 2007).

Conclusion

This article has focused on understanding the conditions under which the strategic decision of groups to pursue rights as 'indigenous peoples' is likely to yield a positive response from the state. The Philippines and Indonesia were two unlikely countries where recognition or institutionalization of diversity would occur. Perhaps more so in Indonesia but also significant in the Philippines, state leaders long sought to centralize their states over federalism or other forms of institutionalizing ethnic differences.

Cordillerans and Papuans strategically cast themselves as nations or as indigenous peoples to obtain special status. Historically, identities as 'Cordilleran' and 'Papuan' were shaped through colonial administration, state policies, and nationalist leaders who sought to construct alternative nations of Cordillerans and Papuans. When the international indigenous peoples' movement emerged, both groups positioned themselves as 'indigenous peoples', with the goals of obtaining some form of self-determination, increased rights to land and resources, and preservation of their unique institutions. In the case of Cordillerans, the pursuit of a pan-Cordilleran identity as a 'nation' never coalesced sufficiently, so activists strategically decided to abandon a nationalist quest and engage fully in the indigenous peoples' movement. Papuans, on the other hand, waivered as they pursued a dual strategy.

Although both made claims as indigenous peoples and mobilized both internationally and domestically, only Cordillerans were successful. The Philippines enshrined indigenous peoples' rights in their constitution and later passed landmark legislation protecting indigenous peoples' rights, whereas Indonesia made no such concessions. The Indonesian government, by closing the door to indigenous peoples' rights, instead opted to use autonomy, which was much more likely to institutionalize Papuans' sense of nationhood. Even though it partially retracted by subsequently dividing the province, nevertheless it symbolically recognized Papuans' status at least as a group needing special recognition. It this sense, it supported Papuans' claims as a sub-state nation.

In both cases, accommodation came at a time of state vulnerability. In the Philippines, concessions to Cordillerans was part of the government's strategy to counter the NPA's ongoing insurgency. In Indonesia, concessions to Papua were partly driven by attempts to find an overall solution to conflicts in East Timor and Aceh, as well as Papua. Autonomy was part of such a strategy, and remained in line with plans for decentralization to regions more generally, without engaging in a greyer realm that indigenous peoples' rights would have entailed.[3]

I have argued, however, that incentives to make concessions do not explain why the Philippines gave recognition and rights as indigenous peoples, while Indonesia did not. Two factors set the Philippines and Indonesia on different paths. First, Cordillerans took advantage of the momentary state weakness and temporarily stronger position of NGOs to mobilize and lobby the constitutional convention. In combination with strong international networks that support these rights, Cordillerans and other indigenous peoples of the Philippines maintained pressure to obtain IPRA, a landmark legislation in the region, after these rights had been constitutionalized. In Indonesia, conversely, Papuans could not create the same kind of international pressure, despite their engagement with the WGIP. Even after democratization, the Indonesian government could continue to shield itself from such pressures by upholding its legislation protecting *adat* and refuting the applicability of international definitions of 'indigenous peoples' in Indonesia. AMAN's attempt to link *adat* to international understandings and networks on indigenous peoples created a new source of domestic pressure on the Indonesian government but has not yet yielded results. At the time of constitutional changes, they were too weak, while Papuans, one of the stronger groups, were both hesitant to advance indigenous peoples' rights rather that their own interests as a separate 'nation'. Most importantly, the space for NGOs and the 'Reformasi' movement was restricted and did not enjoy the kind of access to the constitutional process as Cordillerans momentarily enjoyed in the Philippines.

Other factors contributed to these outcomes as well. Although NGOs and civil society groups did not sustain their lobbying power in the Philippines, nevertheless some administrations, especially under President Fidel Ramos, felt compelled for electoral reasons to articulate a pro-civil society agenda. IPRA resulted in part from these electoral dynamics.

Ethnic groups at times have the choice of positioning themselves as 'nations' or 'indigenous peoples'. They calculate their ability to develop particular alliances internationally and domestically, and the chances that expected gains will meet their expectations. States have generally been more likely to yield on indigenous peoples' rights than on accommodating claims to nationhood. The cases of the Cordillerans and Papuans show the particular importance of timing, where articulating a position at moments of state weakness can create sufficient momentum to constitutionalize indigenous peoples' rights. When such critical junctures are missed, it becomes more difficult to use sustained international and domestic pressure to produce such gains.

Acknowledgements

I would like to thank Michelle Miller and the anonymous reviewers for very useful comments on the original manuscript. I am also grateful for funding from the Social Sciences and Humanities Research Council of Canada as well as the United States Institute of Peace.

Notes

1. See section 22, art. 11; section 5, art. 12; section 6, art. 13.
2. 'Indigenous communities, peoples and nations are those which, having a historical continuity with pre-invasion and pre-colonial societies that developed on their territories, consider themselves distinct from other sectors of the societies now prevailing in those territories, or parts of them. They form at present non-dominant sectors of society and are determined to preserve, develop and transmit to future generations their ancestral territories, and their ethnic identity, as the basis of their continued existence as peoples, in accordance with their own cultural patterns, social institutions and legal systems.' (Martínez Cobo 1986, p. 50)
3. For a recent, different perspective see Walter 2009.

References

ACCIAIOLI, G. 2001 'Grounds of conflict, idioms of harmony: custom, religion, and nationalism in violence avoidance at the Lindu Plain, Central Sulawesi', *Indonesia*, vol. 72, pp. 81–114

AMAN 1999a 'Aman: Indonesia's new indigenous voice', *Down to Earth*, no. 41, May

—— 1999b 'Aman's aims and organization', *Down to Earth*, Special Issue, October

ASPINALL, E. 2005 *Opposing Suharto: Compromise, Resistance, and Regime Change in Indonesia*, Stanford, CA: Stanford University Press

—— 2009 *Islam and nation: Separatist Rebellion in Aceh, Indonesia*, Stanford, CA: Stanford University Press

BARNES, R. H., ANDREW, G. and KINGSBURY, B. 1995 *Indigenous Peoples of Asia*, Ann Arbor, MI: Association for Asian Studies

BERTRAND, J. 2004 *Nationalism and Ethnic Conflict in Indonesia*, New York: Cambridge University Press

—— 2007 'Indonesia's quasi-federalist approach: accommodation amid strong integrationist tendencies', *International Journal of Constitutional Law*, vol. 5, no. 4, pp. 576–605

BERTRAND, J. and LALIBERTÉ, A. 2010 *Multination States in Asia: Accommodation or Resistance*, New York: Cambridge University Press

CASTRO, N. T. 2000 'Three years of the Indigenous Peoples' Rights Act: its impact on indigenous communities', *Kasarinlan*, vol. 15, no. 2, pp. 35–54

CHAUVEL, R. 2005 'Constructing Papuan nationalism: history, ethnicity, and adaptation', in *History, Ethnicity, and Adaptation Policy Studies 14*, Washington, DC: East West Center

CONSTITUTION INDONESIA 2006 *Constitution of the Republic of Indonesia 1945 (with amendments), [Undang-Undang Dasar Republik Indonesia 1945]*

CWIS 1984 'Review of recent developments in the Cordillera provinces: Northern Luzon', statement to the UN Working Group on Indigenous Populations, Center for World Indigenous Studies

—— 1985a 'Statement by Mr Juwana, Observer of the Republic of Indonesia', UN Working Group on Indigenous Populations of the Sub-Commission on Prevention of Discrimination and Protection of Minorities, fourth session, 1 August, Fourth World Documentation Project, Center for World Indigenous Studies

—— 1985b 'Statement on behalf of the Papuan people', UN Working Group on Indigenous Populations, fourth session, July–August, Fourth World Documentation Project, Center for World Indigenous Studies

DAES, E.-I. 2000 'Protection of the world's indigenous peoples and human rights', in J. Symonides (ed.), *Human Rights: Concept and Standards*, Aldershot: Ashgate

DAVIDSON, J. S. and HENLEY, D. 2007 *The Revival of Tradition in Indonesian Politics: The Deployment of Adat from Colonialism to Indigenism*, London: Routledge

DEFERT, G. 1996 *L'Indonésie et la Nouvelle-Guinée-Occidentale: maintien des frontières coloniales ou respect des identités communautaires*, Paris: Editions l'Harmattan

DUNCAN, C. R. 2004 'From development to empowerment: changing Indonesian government policies toward indigenous minorities', in C. R. Duncan (ed.), *Civilizing the Margins: Southeast Asian Government Policies for the Development of Minorities*, Ithaca, NJ: Cornell University Press

ELSHAM 2003 'Statement under the auspices of the UN Working Group on Minorities: the West Papuan case', UN Working Group on Minorities, ninth Session, May, United Nations Commission on Human Rights, Sub-Commission on the Promotion and Protection of Human Rights

FININ, G. A. 2005 *The Making of the Igorot: Contours of Cordillera Consciousness*, Quezon City: Ateneo de Manila Press

FREE PAPUA MOVEMENT 1984 'Statement on behalf of the Free Papua Movement', UN Working Group on Indigenous Populations, third Session, 30 July–3 August, Fourth World Documentation Project, Center for World Indigenous Studies

HOWARD, B. R. 2003 *Indigenous Peoples snd the State: The Struggle for Native Rights*, DeKalb, IL: Northern Illinois University Press

HYNDMAN, D. 1991 'Organic act rejected in the Cordillera: dialects of a continuing fourth world autonomy movement in the Philippines', *Dialectical Anthropology*, vol. 16, no. 2, pp. 169–84

KING, B. 2001 'Constitutional tinkering: the search for consensus is taking time', *Inside Indonesia*, vol. 65, Jan–March http://www.insideindonesia.org/edition-65/constitutional-tinkering [accessed 15 December 2010]

—— 2004 'Empowering the presidency: interests and perceptions in Indonesia's constitutional reforms, 1999–2002', PhD dissertation, Department of Political Science, Ohio State University, Columbus, OH

KING, P. 2002 'Morning star rising? Indonesia Raya and the new Papuan nationalism', *Indonesia*, vol. 73, pp. 89–127

—— 2005 'West Papua and Indonesia since Suharto: independence, autonomy or chaos?', *Contemporary Southeast Asia*, vol. 27, no. 1, pp. 151–3

KINGSBURY, B. 1995 '"Indigenous Peoples" as an international legal concept', in R. H. Barnes, G. Andrew and B. Kingsbury (eds), *Indigenous Peoples of Asia*, Ann Arbor, MI: Association for Asian Studies

—— 1999 'The applicability of the international legal concept of "indigenous peoples" in Asia', in J. R. Bauer and D. Bell (eds), *The East Asian Challenge for Human Rights*, Cambridge: Cambridge University Press

LAGERBERG, K. 1979 *West Irian and Jakarta Imperialism*, New York: St. Martin's Press

LI, T. 2000 'Constituting tribal space: indigenous identity and resource politics in Indonesia', *Comparative Studies in Society and History*, vol. 42, no. 1, p. 149

LI, T. M. 2001 'Masyarakat adat, difference, and the limits of recognition in Indonesia's forest zone', *Modern Asian Studies*, vol. 35, no. 3, pp. 645–76

LIDDLE, R. W. 1999 'Indonesia's democratic opening', *Government and Opposition*, vol. 34, no. 1, p. 94

LIJPHART, A. 1966 *The Trauma of Decolonization: The Dutch and West New* Guinea, New Haven, CT: Yale University Press

LP3BH 2004 'The West Papua case', statement by Yan Christian Warinussy, UN Working Group on Minorities, tenth session, March, United Nations Commission on Human Rights, Sub-Commission on the Promotion and Protection of Human Rights

MANDOWEN, W. 2005 'West Papua and the right to self-determination: a challenge to human rights', in T. Rathgeber (ed.), *Economic, Social and Cultural Rights in West Papua: A Study on Social Reality and Political Perspectives*, Evangelical Church in the Rhineland, Wuppertal: Foedus-Verlag

MARTÍNEZ COBO, J. 1986 'Study of the problem of discrimination against indigenous populations' (Chapter 21 Conclusions, proposals and recommendations. UN Doc. No. E/CN.4 Sub.2/1983/21/ADD.8), Geneva: United Nations

MCKENNA, T. M. 1998 *Muslim Rulers and Rebels: Everyday Politics and Armed Separatism in the Southern Philippines*, Berkeley, CA: University of California Press

MORGAN, R. 2004 'Advancing indigenous rights at the United Nations: strategic framing and its impact on the normative development of international law', *Social Legal Studies*, vol. 13, no. 4, p. 481

—— 2007 'On political institutions and social movement dynamics: the case of the United Nations and the global indigenous movement', *International Political Science Review*, vol. 28, no. 3, pp. 273–92

MORRIS, E. E. 1985 'Aceh under the new order', *Indonesia Reports*, vol. 6, 20 April, pp. 1–6

MOTE, O. and RUTHERFORD, D. 2001 'From Irian Jaya to Papua: the limits of primordialism in Indonesia's troubled east', *Indonesia*, vol. 72, pp. 115–40

NIEZEN, R. 2003 *The Origins of Indigenism: Human Rights and the Politics of Identity*, Berkeley, CA: University of California Press

ETHNIC AND RACIAL MINORITIES IN ASIA

OSBORNE, R. 1985 *Indonesia's Secret War: The Guerilla Struggle in Irian Jaya*, Allen &
Unwin
PRILL-BRETT, J. 1994 "Indigenous land rights and legal pluralism among Philippine
highlanders", *Law and Society Review*, vol. 28, no. 3, pp. 687–97, 707–20
ROOD, S. 1987 *Issues on Cordillera Autonomy: Conference Proceedings*, Baguio City:
Cordillera Studies Center, University of the Philippines College Baguio
––––– 1991 'Issues on creating an autonomous region for the Cordillera, Northern
Philippines', *Ethnic and Racial Studies*, vol. 14, no. 4, pp. 516–44
SANDERS, D. 1989 'The UN Working Group on Indigenous Populations", *Human Rights
Quarterly*, vol. 11, no. 3, pp. 406–33
STAVENHAGEN, R. 2004 'Mission to the Philippines: Addendum to the Report of the
Special Rapporteur on the situation of human rights and fundamental freedoms of
indigenous people', United Nations General Assembly
TAPOL 1984 *West Papua: The Obliteration of a People*, London: Tapol
UN CERD 2006 'Indonesia, Addendum, Third periodic report of States Parties Due in
2000', United Nations International Convention on the Elimination of all Forms of Racial
Discrimination
UN ESC 2004 'Provisional summary record of the 48th meeting, UN Economic and Social
Council'
WALTER, B. F. 2009 *Reputation and Civil War: Why Separatist Conflicts are So Violent*,
Cambridge: Cambridge University Press
WEBSTER, D. 2002 'Already sovereign as a people": a foundational moment in West
Papuan nationalism", *Pacific Affairs*, vol. 74, no. 4, pp. 507–28

118

Index

INDEX

Webster, D. 101
Wee, W. 64
Welsch, W. 67
West New Guinea 105; Irian Jaya 105–6
West Papua 15, 18–23, 51
West Papua National Coalition for
  Liberation (WPNCL) 22–3
White Paper on Shared Values (1991) 75
Willford, A.: Bunnell, T. and Najarajan,
  S. 57
Willmott, W. 33
Wongthes, Suchit 87

World Bank 3; transmigration
  programme 106
Wright, T. 51

Yack, B. 53–4
Young, I. 50, 84
Yurdakul, G.: Bloemraad, I. and
  Korteweg, A. 55
Yusuf, I. 83

Zoohri, W. 73

For Product Safety Concerns and Information please contact our EU
representative GPSR@taylorandfrancis.com
Taylor & Francis Verlag GmbH, Kaufingerstraße 24, 80331 München, Germany

www.ingramcontent.com/pod-product-compliance
Lightning Source LLC
Chambersburg PA
CBHW050534270326
41926CB00015B/3225